Light Into Dawn
– Randy's Miracle

Bethel Chang

Bethel chang 6/4/99

Edited by Jack Turner, Ph.D.
Translation Assisted by Catherine Chang, Ph.D.
(From the previous Chinese publication,
Child of Oriental Face)

Publisher:
Mimosa Ministry, Inc.
355 Mimosa Ave.
Dover, Delaware 19904

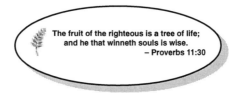

The fruit of the righteous is a tree of life;
and he that winneth souls is wise.
– Proverbs 11:30

Dover Litho Printing Company
Dover, Delaware

Book Design by
Franklin D. Arbaugh
Dover, Delaware

Cover Design by Franklin D. Arbaugh
Front Cover photograph courtesy of National Geographic
World, Richard T Howitz, Photographer
Back Cover photograph by Franklin D. Arbaugh

Printed in the United States of America

ISBN 0-9669393-0-1

Dedication

To the honor and glory of God,
- for He loves us so much and provides us with our
  daily strength.

To my three sons, Geoffrey, Isaac, and Randy,
- may the Lord bless you for the hearts that love one
  another.

To my dear husband, Clement,
- for your love, encouragement and comfort;
-without your company, life's journey would be so
  much harder.

Acknowledgments

While I was waiting in the long line at the "Journey into Imagination" at Disney World, I saw a slogan painted on the wall. It said, "Our environment is like a patchwork quilt. Each 'patch' is dependent on those around it. If one part unravels, it affects the rest." How true it is! Each one of us is a synergized result of many components encountered in his or her life. Those components are inter-related and inter-woven into the "patchwork" that miraculously represents an individual.

I am grateful for the wisdom and inspiration of many men and women, who have helped me sustain my faith and have given me encouragement along the winding road of my life. I call them "the messengers from God."

For the development of this book, I feel a deep sense of gratitude to:

- ❧ the board members of the Mimosa Ministry, Inc., whose faithfulness, prayers, and consultations have encouraged me to continue my difficult task. They are the sounding boards and timekeepers for the project;
- ❧ my dear husband, Clement, and our two older children, Geoffrey and Isaac, for your tremendous patience and support;
- ❧ my third child, Randy, for he has walked with me in the process of learning three very important lessons, those of faith, hope, and love;
- ❧ my dear sister-in-law, Catherine Chang, whose commitment and help were vital for the translation;

- Jack Turner, my gifted editor and advisor, who suggested the idea of this project to me before the thought had even entered my mind;
- Nancy Hawk, the President of American Mothers, Inc., for her encouragement and taking the time to write the preface;
- Franklin D. Arbaugh, for the beautiful design of the book cover; and
- Trish Morton, for your efforts in assisting me in the printing process.

Editor's Note

I've edited so many books that I've lost count, but I do know that this book is one of the few I'll remember, one of the few I consider really important. The project came along at a good time for me, because it came along at a bad time in my life. I was at a personal low point, and I don't know exactly why. My attitude was bitter, even though I had lots to be happy about.

Then my friend Bethel Chang casually mentioned one day that she had written a book in Chinese about her special son Randy, and I suggested that she get it translated and published in English. She wondered if I would be interested in editing the translation. "Sure," I said. "Why not? I'd love to read your book anyway." (I have always liked Bethel because she is a genuinely good person; she is like sunlight on a cloudy day.)

Once I started editing her book, my attitude toward life began to change. I realized that whatever my problems were, they paled in comparison to the ordeal Bethel and her family had endured – and had come through with emotional and spiritual strength and renewal. My admiration for them lifted my spirits. I began to get into the story and to look forward to my editing sessions. I wanted to find out what happened to this special child, and I wanted to learn exactly how his parents had dealt with the problems as well as the miracles that seemed to happen almost daily. What an emotional roller-coaster it must have been for them! Yet, for the most part, they maintained their equanimity, their dignity, and their strong love for each other and for their children.

Their story reconnected me with the most important things in life and showed me how much one can accomplish with faith, love, and joyful effort. I am proud and grateful to have been involved with such a worthwhile project.

This honest little book has a lot to say. Please allow yourself to hear it.

– Jack Turner, Ph.D.

Foreword

One night, after my mom finished writing this book, I took her draft to my room to read. At first, I was only curious about the story of myself. Before long, I was totally engrossed in it.

At 1:30 A.M., I was still reading. My mom came to my room. She wondered why I was still up. I turned to her, hugged her, and said to her, "Mom, I was certainly born different, wasn't I? Not only I was different, I was a difficult baby for you and Dad."

For all these years, people called me a "Down's Syndrome" person, and my parents told me that I had many surgeries when I was a baby. But not until that night had I realized that my parents had cried so much for me when I was young.

Despite all the problems I had, Dad and Mom did a wonderful job in raising and teaching me. Mom always can find a way to help me. She always said that she has a magic way to "transfer" her knowledge to me. She is certainly a great teacher. Dad's classical music collection turned every dinnertime in my home into a concert hall. He always saves the sport page for me and is my ally in the football season.

I also learned from my parents that by connecting myself to the source of wisdom, the Creator, I could receive abilities beyond my own disabilities. I also understand that, though I am imperfect, God created me with a perfect plan. My life was spared for a purpose.

I can never repay the love and effort Dad and Mom put in for me. But I know that their hearts will be satisfied if I do my best and share God's blessings with others.

God bless you Dad and Mom. I love you very much.

- Randy Chang

Preface

The Chang family is truly remarkable, as all who read this book will learn. Bethel Chang tells the story of how she, her husband, and their two older sons coped with a Down's Syndrome child, born more than a decade after their second son. With two boys who are academically brilliant and musically talented, Clement and Bethel Chang were not prepared for a Down's Syndrome child.

Bethel's frank and straightforward description of her despair is a gripping story. She is so expressive that the reader aches as she aches, cringes as she cringes, sobs as she sobs. Bethel finally accepted reality and placed their future in God's hands. Then she determined to do everything possible to help this child reach his fullest potential. That meant immediate and active work, finding suitable help in the community for Randy, everyone in the family helping with his exercises and training, constant positive reinforcement of any of his efforts, and continuous moral support for Randy and for each other.

All three of the boys reveal their parent's love and commitment to excellence. Geoffrey, the oldest, is a Ph.D. from the University of Pennsylvania Medical School and an accomplished scientist. He plays the clarinet beautifully, having performed with American Youth in Concert in Carnegie Hall and several European countries. Isaac, the middle son, is a Ph.D. from the University of Pennsylvania Bio-medical Engineering School. He works for the FDA and already holds multiple patents on heart catheter designs. Isaac won an international young pianist contest when he was 18 and performed as a soloist for the Delaware Symphony Orchestra in the Wilmington Grand

Opera House. Randy, the youngest, the Down's Syndrome and legally blind child, is in high school, mainstreamed, doing well in his studies, and plays piano with enthusiasm and grace.

Because the way in which she has mothered her boys had led each to his highest potential, Bethel was chosen the Delaware Mother of the Year in 1998 by the Delaware Association of American Mothers, Inc. American Mothers is the official sponsor of Mothers Day, and its purpose is the strengthening of the moral and spiritual foundations of the family and the home. To find a family such as the Changs', with strong moral and spiritual values apparent to any observation, a model for others, is most rewarding for American Mothers. For the Changs to have their efforts recognized is a much-deserved honor and acknowledgment of the good results of their years of struggle.

– Nancy D. Hawk, President, American Mothers, Inc.

Table of Contents

The Chang family:
Geoffrey, Isaac, Randy, Bethel, and Clement

First performance at age 10, Dover, Delaware

Strike the last note with brother Isaac at
National Developmental Disabilities Convention.

Randy and his piano teacher, Tracy Richardson
at the Wilmington Music School.

SEND HER TO ANOTHER ROOM

Motherhood is a laborious job, but it is usually gratifying and sometimes very much so. There is no denying, though, that it starts with labor.

After receiving lots of advice from medical professionals and many other mothers, I decided to take a challenge, to experience fully the adventure of childbirth – a natural birth in the Lamaze style.

After twenty-six hours of labor, I was finally able to cuddle the cute and chubby baby in my arms. I enjoyed the happiest moment of motherhood in the recovery room of the hospital. Though he was my third child, the inner satisfaction wasn't a bit suppressed.

The baby was beautiful. I couldn't believe his eyes were open when the nurse handed him to me. His cheeks were pink and his little tongue was licking his lips. His complexion was fair, and his hair was dark. What a beautiful and adorable baby! I certainly regretted that I missed the opportunity to be a "Lamaze mom" for my two older boys. The effects of anesthesia during their births had made me semiconscious and erased all memory of the birth process.

"Randy! Randy!" my husband, Clement, said to the new baby. "This is your mommy. I am your daddy!" Clement was just as tired as I was, but he was overwhelmingly excited by the experience. Even before he took off his surgical gown and mask, he started to teach our newborn his own name and those of his family members.

I could tell that my husband was proud and excited

about being a witness to the birth of our son. Using the telephone in the recovery room, he began to inform our family and friends of the happy news.

Everything seemed to be so lovely. I finally and truly understood the meaning of this passage in the Bible: "A woman giving birth to a child has pain because her time has come; but when her baby is born she forgets the anguish because of her joy that a child is born into the world."

About an hour later the head nurse came and politely told me that I would be sent to a regular patient's room. As a nurse was taking me to my apparently assigned double room, I heard the head nurse calling after her:

"No! No! Not that room. Send her to another room."

"Why? Do I have the wrong room number? Are you sure it isn't this room?" The nurse paused to verify the room number on the slip.

"No! No!" the head nurse answered in a commanding tone.

"What shall I do now?" the nurse asked.

"Send her to the other room." The head nurse pointed to an empty single room.

"That room is empty. Didn't we agree to send her to a double room?"

"Just listen to me. I have a reason for it. Please, trust me and take my word for now," the head nurse calmly said to the nurse.

The nurses apparently thought a happy, Asian mother like me wouldn't pay any attention to their conversation. But I heard it all.

Silently I began to question "Why" and what was in

the mind of the head nurse. Then I told myself to forget it and not to let the suspicious thoughts spoil my joyful day.

After getting me settled, the two nurses left and closed the door. I looked around the spacious room and thought how kind the head nurse was to put me here by myself. I could surely enjoy some quietness in recuperation.

Clement came in and looked tired. I told him to go home and tell the older boys about their cute and adorable kid brother.

For a long while there wasn't anyone coming in to see me as I was resting quietly. The door was tightly shut. The voice of the head nurse echoed in my mind: "Take her to another room… I have a reason for it… trust me… take my word for now."

AN EMERGENCY AND AN EMPTY BED

The door opened. A pediatrician walked in with my newborn baby in his arms; a nurse followed him. He appeared sober and concerned. With a serious tone he said, "Mrs. Chang, I have to tell you that there are some problems with your baby." I tried to keep myself calm, but my heart was pounding heavily. "The baby was born with an imperforate anus – he does not have a normal opening on his bottom. We have to take him to the Wilmington Medical Center right away because this hospital doesn't have the required facilities to help him. A medical helicopter has been requested. Mrs. Chang, do you have any questions?"

Questions? My questions? Regarding the baby's medical conditions or whether we should send him to a larger hospital? I was so stunned with this unexpected situation that I can't recall how the conversation ended. They left the door ajar as they took the baby away.

I was so anxious to let Clement know this unfortunate news and must have tried dozens of times to phone home but couldn't get through. He was on the phone calling relatives and friends about our newborn baby!

My heart sank like a rock in deep water. Fear had crept into that lonely and empty room; I've never been so frightened in my life. Feeling helpless and fearful, I wanted to cry but couldn't. Instead, I just stared at the blank white ceiling. Subconsciously I heard a voice whispering: "Why don't you pray?" But I couldn't utter a word of prayer either.

In this state of confusion, I heard a baby crying out in

the hallway; it must have been feeding time. Nurses usually handed babies to their mothers. Where was my baby? I wanted to hold him. Where was he?

I got up and walked toward the nursery. Looking through the large window I didn't see my Randy at first. Was he gone? Where was his crib? After a bit of searching, I found him. He had been placed in a separate room, too, and the room was not connected to the regular nursery. Through a door and through another door I finally found a way to see my baby more closely through a window. The little chubby baby with pink cheeks was sound asleep. I cried and murmured, "I know you don't know what's ahead of you. Mommy has no idea of that either."

With tears running down my face, I slowly dragged myself back to my room. Oddly, no one seemed to have seen me, or maybe I just didn't see anyone around.

Finally, the phone line was clear. At first I pretended to be calm and told Clement that our child had problems. Then the sorrow and sadness within me broke like a dam. Tears flooded the phone receiver and the pillow as I was explaining the sad news to him.

Later the doctor and nurse came in with my baby. "Mrs. Chang, we were unable to get hold of the medical helicopter because it is being used to transport people injured in an accident. We'll take your baby to the Wilmington Medical Center in an ambulance. We'll leave as soon as your husband gets here. Why don't you hold the baby and enjoy him for a while as we get the ambulance ready?" The nurse laid the baby by my side, and she and the doctor left, both of them smiling at me.

5

Light Into Dawn – Randy's Miracle

I tried to enjoy the short time we were together then, recalling the excitement in holding Randy for the first time. Even though he was my third child, the mother/child relationship always remained as close as that with the two older boys. Little Randy had his eyes open; I touched his face and tiny hands – how cute and adorable! I wanted to stare at him as much as possible, knowing that he may not look the same the next time I saw him. Maybe he would safely survive the operation or he might lose weight on account of unforeseen hardships. He might end up with all kinds of tubing in him. He may.... The more I thought about these things, I couldn't stop crying while holding him close to me. I told myself not to waste time crying; yet who could comfort me at this moment?

The doctor and nurse came back to my room and were followed by Clement. He wore a surgical uniform and was looking pale and exhausted. I knew he was as tired, fearful, anxious, and helpless as I was.

"Mrs. Chang, the ambulance is ready outside. Let me hold the baby," the nurse said as she walked toward me. Suddenly I started to hold Randy very tightly; I really didn't want to let him go. I couldn't believe what was before me. Tears of anguish poured out again; then I heard Clement's voice: "Please be reasonable, Bethel. Don't cry. Our child needs help." I finally let go, and the baby was taken away.

This was indeed a terrible and lonesome night. The nurse gave me two sleeping pills. I asked her repeatedly to let me know how Randy was doing, and she promised me that she would keep me posted on his operation at the Wilmington Medical Center.

6

An Emergency and an Empty Bed

I didn't fall asleep even after taking the sleeping pills, which only made my eyelids feel heavy. My mind was still wide awake, however. Anxiety seemed to have deprived me of having a restful night much needed after the agonizing labor and the events that followed Randy's birth. My thoughts had gone with the ambulance and remained with my baby. From the bottom of my heart I cried out to God for help in easing my pain.

About two o'clock in the morning the kind nurse quietly came in. I couldn't wait to ask her: "Did the ambulance get to Wilmington? Is there any news yet?" She told me in a tender voice that things had gone smoothly and that Clement was with Randy all the time. As soon as the ambulance arrived at the Wilmington Medical Center, the baby had been immediately transferred to the infant emergency center.

Feeling somewhat comforted, I tried to close my eyes and get to sleep. Suddenly, the head nurse's voice echoed in my ears once again: "Send her to another room! Do as I told you! I have a reason for it. Trust me."

I began to realize that when Randy was born, the head nurse recognized the unfortunate situation. She didn't want the mother to share a room with another patient. I was grateful for her thoughtfulness; however, it also provoked many more questions: how many abnormal problems did Randy have? Were they deliberately keeping these problems from me? How did I end up with an abnormal baby?

Frightening thoughts and guilty feelings brewed within me. I got to the point of losing my mind. I heard my own spontaneous crying yet wasn't able to stop it; neither could

I move my numb hands and feet. I heard someone screaming but couldn't discern where it came from. It was already late at night; I forgot the patients in the neighboring rooms were sound asleep. I started yelling to God: "Oh God, I told you before that I could never handle a handicapped child. Why did you give me a defective baby? Why are you so unfair?" In the midst of confusion and sadness, I argued with God, sometimes screaming, at times just murmuring to myself. I was terrified at the thought of losing control of my mind, even though I have always considered myself to be a very "rational" person.

The next two days went by in a mixture of good and bad moods. I was puzzled over why the doctor and the nurse didn't come in to check on me. Only staff members came to bring in three meals, took blood samples, and changed the bed linen. They all seemed to have been told to close the door as they were leaving my room.

The pastor of our church visited me. He read a passage from the Bible to comfort me and offered a short prayer. I thanked him for his kindness.

On the third evening, Clement came back with his mother and sister and brought beautiful flowers. They looked tired but smiled. I had to smile back as they told me not to worry, just to try to rest up and recuperate, since everything was progressing smoothly. I noticed Clement had a blood-shot right eye, which he blamed on lack of sleep. (Poor fellow! He had to drive back and forth between Dover and Wilmington again and again. After visiting me, he would go home and drive to the Wilmington Medical Center to be with Randy the next morning.) Their visit cheered me up somewhat. However, shortly after their departure, my depression set in again.

I began to get homesick and thought about our older sons at home, the healthy nine and ten year olds. They had been patiently waiting for the arrival of their little brother or sister and enjoyed placing their ears and hands on my tummy to feel the baby's heartbeat or kicks; especially our second son, Isaac, born with extremely sensitive ears – he could discern and count the baby's heartbeats without using a stethoscope. Now the baby brother had been born but couldn't go home as expected for them to see. What a disappointment and loss to the big brothers! I wanted to go home! I wanted Randy to go home!

I pressed the "call" button to send for the nurse on duty. As soon as she came to the door, I said to her, "Will you ask the doctor if I can go home tomorrow morning? I want to go home. I have to go home. Will you please find the doctor!"

The doctor did let me go home the next day. As I entered the front door, a strange and empty feeling crawled inside me. I had left there with a big belly three days ago – just like two previous pregnancies, which ended up with me happily accompanying the newborn babies home and putting them in their cribs. What a joyous moment to be home at those times! But this time, things were quite different.

Randy's crib was empty but with the sheets and comforter neatly in place. All kinds of baby gifts filled the closet. I had spent many evenings carefully decorating the baby's room and had also tarried countless hours in the room waiting and thinking of his arrival. Now the time had come, yet he couldn't come home to enjoy what we'd prepared for him.

The two older boys stared at me apparently with many questions. I tried hard to keep myself calm and rational and reminded them not to forget to pray for their baby brother. I thought my years of experience in the business world had trained me to be stress-resistant and self-reliant, the characteristics I desperately needed to display to the boys.

Since early childhood I always wanted to be the person "in control." Even though I was an only child, as a girl I reminded myself that I should behave like a boy – to be tough when things were rough and should not cry in front of people. For the sake of my parents and my boys, I concealed my pain and suppressed my emotions so that they wouldn't detect the seriousness of the situation. The only person who would listen to my complaints was Clement; however, we were both in a similar situation.

Who could understand and ease the pain in my heart? In the quietness of the night I often poured out my grief that had accumulated during the day and let the tears run and soak my pillow. "Randy! Randy!" I cried. "Mommy misses you very much. When can you come home?"

Recalling those miserable days, I feel that I was really selfish to think about my own pain. I didn't know much about Randy's problems and what was in store for us in the future. Clement was the one who bore much heavier burdens than I did in those times, but I did not learn the details until later.

CHILD OF ORIENTAL FACE

In the dreadful and heart-breaking night that Randy was taken away in an ambulance to the Wilmington Medical Center, his father – sitting in an ambulance for the first time in his life – stared at the infant lying in the incubator. Clement was tired, puzzled, and he felt helpless. The vehicle sped towards Wilmington Medical Center, fifty miles away from Dover.

The ambulance had subdued interior lighting, very soothing to patients, and the emergency crew members were not only well trained and efficient but also courteous and ready to serve whenever they were called upon. Clement thanked them for their help.

The Wilmington Medical Center had prepared for the arrival of this young patient. A nurse from the Infant Intensive Care Unit (IICU) transferred him from the ambulance's incubator to the hospital room.

After admitting Randy into the hospital, Clement waited anxiously for the pediatrician. He felt that he was surrounded by a strange environment. Some unfamiliar medical terms came to his mind. Across the room, there were two tiny two-pound, palm-sized twins, wearing white hats, being treated for jaundice. Next to Randy, a newborn baby girl had been diagnosed with a cleft palate. Diagonally across from him, a baby boy lay with at least forty wires coming out of his little body. The nurse said that he was born with his stomach hanging outside his body. "Will our Randy look like one of them, with all the tubes and wires attached to him? Will he survive? Where are the parents of these unfortunate children? How do they cope with the situation?" Clement asked himself, as his heart twisted with pain and pity.

"Mr. Chang, Dr. Minor wants to see you," a nurse said to him.

"I am Dr. Minor, Pediatric Surgeon," said a tall man around fifty.

"Hello, Dr. Minor. Thank you for answering the call at 1:00 A.M. I really appreciate your help." Clement shook Dr. Minor's hand and asked, "What is my Randy's problem?"

Rather than a surgeon, Dr. Minor looked more like a Catholic priest. He was dressed in a long gray gown with a white collar and had a wooden cross hanging on his chest. He talked softly and low. His large hands, which seemed way too big to work on tiny babies, held together in front of his cross, as if he were praying all the time.

"Do not worry, Mr. Chang," said Dr. Minor. "Randy is doing okay at this moment. You are at the right place, and this is the best we can do for now. I need to have some X-rays done and order a few lab tests so I can obtain some data about this baby before we can figure out the next step. I will do my best to help him and will pray to God to give me the wisdom to help him."

Dr. Minor seemed so gentle in his heart, so candid and sincere in his word, and so humble in his mind that Clement could not help but ask about his religious background.

"Dr. Minor, are you a Catholic Father?"

"No, I am not. But I am a Catholic. I have volunteered myself for a Christian medical ministry for a few years.

God has used my hands to heal many infants. He has blessed His healing through me. I always ask Him to be my partner in the operating room."

Therefore, we began to call him "Father Doctor Minor." He definitely looked more like a Father than a doctor to us.

He spent the next few minutes telling Clement about some preliminary findings.

Randy's problem, medically, is called an "imperforate anus," which is not all that rare for a newborn baby. During one stage of fetal development, the lower section of his colon had developed abnormally. Consequently no bottom opening was formed. Of course, this abnormality prevented the body from performing the necessary excretion process, and was detrimental to the baby's survival. Babies born with this condition had been helpless and usually died in a few days prior to the advent of modern medical technology.

Dr. Minor explained, "There are two possible ways to solve the problem, and they totally depend on the x-ray report. If the ending of the colon is low enough, we can work from the bottom, and try to pull down the colon and connect it to the opening. If the ending is, unfortunately, too 'high,' then I would have to implement a colostomy, which may stay with him for a few years until he is at least three years old. Then another medical procedure will be needed to close the colostomy, open his bottom, and reconnect the colon."

Dr. Minor continued, "When I was a young doctor many years ago, I was not as experienced. I had a good heart and anxiously wanted to save infants' lives. I made

13

quick decisions based on medical and academic knowledge. I implanted colostomies for several babies, and then, a couple of years later, I performed the second corrective surgery. Actually, as my experience increased, I learned that the location of the ending of the colon can actually move lower in the first few days of a baby's life. I wish I had waited a little longer for some of my patients, who were on the borderline of 'high' and 'low.' I could have saved some of the babies from going through the surgery twice and may have saved much worry for their parents. I have learned that patience is critical for both anxious doctors and parents. The observation for the first seventy-two hours is absolutely important."

The x-ray later showed that Randy was exactly in this "border" range. Dr. Minor encouraged Clement to pray for the miracle to happen.

Clement spent the night at his sister's house in Wilmington and returned to the Wilmington Medical Center the next morning. Dr. Minor had arrived earlier and was studying Randy's x-ray report when Clement walked in.

"The ending of the colon is shifting lower!" he reported excitedly. "Praise the Lord! You have listened to your servant's prayer!" It sounded as if Dr. Minor were talking to himself. Clement was really moved by his sincerity and faithfulness. Dr. Minor was truly a good doctor with his patient in mind.

"Randy is in no immediate danger," he said. "We need to be patient. Give him a little bit more time. Maybe the ending will get even lower."

Patience! Patience! It is the hardest thing in the world. It is always too long for the person who is waiting. It makes the mind suffer, every minute, every second.

Time passed slowly. Clement's eyes stared at Randy constantly. He worried about his wife and children: "Oh, Lord, how lonely is Bethel at this moment? Is she terrified by the unknown? How are the other two boys doing back home? Will our Randy survive?"

The next x-ray report indicated that there was no more shifting for Randy's colon. Dr. Minor examined him over and over. Then he called Clement and his sister to the side. Diplomatically and tactfully, he said, "Mr. Chang, I feel that I must tell you something, which is very important."

"Yes, Dr. Minor, please," said Clement.

"Your son is a little special. Well, he is a little bit different from other normal children," said Dr. Minor very carefully.

"Of course, I understand. You have told me that he is a child with an imperforate anus. You have examined his x-ray report so many times, and you have been working for him since last night. I understand the problem you described to me." Clement tried to ensure Dr. Minor that he appreciated his efforts.

"Well, Mr. Chang, I think he has a problem which is even more special than just the imperforate anus."

Clement and his sister looked at each other.

"Really?" asked Clement.

"I feel that this child has… a bit of an 'oriental' look."

"Oh! Dr. Minor, of course he has. I am Chinese. My wife is Chinese. Of course my children are Chinese. Wouldn't you say so?" answered Clement suspiciously. He tried to read the doctor's mind between words.

Dr. Minor realized that these two tired people standing in front of him were weary, puzzled, and were definitely not getting the hint.

"Mr. Chang, have you heard of something called… Down's Syndrome?"

"To tell you the truth, no, I have never…. What is Down's Syndrome? Please, please, spell it for me…. Excuse me, please… I don't know this terminology at all." Clement felt embarrassed and frightened.

"D. O. W. N. apostrophe S… S. Y. N. D. R. O M. E."

On a piece of paper, Clement wrote these two words carefully.

Then Dr. Minor asked, "Have you heard of something called… Mongoloid?"

"Yes, I have. But that was in Chinese history. Dr. Minor, you know all Chinese originated from Mongolia; at least that was the assumption in history or of anthropologists." Clement didn't really know much about what he was saying.

Dr. Minor was convinced at this point that Randy's father had no understanding about this medical term and that he required a further explanation.

"Mr. Chang, let me tell you what it is. Down's Syndrome is a kind of genetic disorder. Its disordered gene is in every cell of the baby. It is a lifelong disorder. There is no medicine that can cure and change the condition. It was discovered by Dr. Down. Therefore, it is named after him."

He continued, "All Down's Syndrome babies have similar traits. Regardless of their ethnic origin, they all carry a somewhat oriental look. That is why some doctors called them 'Mongoloid' in the earlier years. Many Down's Syndrome babies are born with some kind of organ disorder. For example, one third of them have heart defects. Some have urinary or intestinal tract disorders, as in Randy's case. Some of them are fortunate enough to be born without any internal organ disorder."

He paused for a moment. Then, he made the most difficult announcement. "Unfortunately, Mr. Chang, they are mentally retarded and low functioners. Mr. Chang, I certainly hope my preliminary diagnosis is wrong. I hope a further lab test will tell us that I am wrong. But I think my ideas have a certain degree of validity. I must order a genetic lab study to determine the truth."

Dr. Minor stopped. There was a silence.

Finally Clement asked, "Doctor, what can I do now?"

Gently Dr. Minor gave his advice. "You are tired. Go home and rest for a few hours, Mr. Chang. I will keep my eyes on this baby. I will pray for him. The good Lord may lower his colon ending a little bit more. I must correct his problem within seventy-two hours. Most likely I will operate on him tomorrow. If any emergency measures must be taken tonight, I will call you."

Heavy hearted, silently, Clement and his sister left the hospital, discussing in detail everything that Dr. Minor had said.

Down's Syndrome? Down's Syndrome? What is it, they wondered. What kind of disease is it? Why does the genetic disorder have something to do with the intestinal tract disorder? Is Randy a "vegetable" of a person? What exactly is "mentally retarded"?

17

Light Into Dawn – Randy's Miracle

Clement later told his mother, who lives with Clement's sister, about the problems. Then he looked in the dictionary, encyclopedia, and medical guide. What is DOWN'S SYNDROME?

Meanwhile Clement's mother calmly kneeled down and prayed. Clement and his sister soon joined her.

Clement cried aloud. This was the most painful prayer he had uttered in his life. He lay face down on the floor and cried his heart out to God. He felt his chest was bursting with twisted pain, and his head seemed swollen with the pressure inside. "Why? Why, Lord, why did you give us a strange baby like this? Lord, why have you given us so much pain in our lives?" He repeated the prayer again and again.

His mother cried. His sister cried. The three of them holding each other, they continued to cry. They cried to God for the unfair fate given to Randy. They cried for Randy's two brothers. Why did they have to endure such trouble in their young lives? And they cried for Randy's mother. "Oh, Lord," said Clement. "How can she take this news?"

Their tears were tinged with anger and with a sadness that could never have been imagined. They cried for hours – without hope, without comfort, and without strength.

Exhausted and looking at the mirror, Clement could hardly recognize himself. His eyes were swollen, and the right eye was bloody red. He was stunned by looking at his own face, and he was frightened. He thought about his wife, recovering from the rough delivery at the hospital in Dover. "How am I going to tell her?" he wondered to himself. "Can she take it? Should I hide the news from her? And how long can I hide it from her?" For a moment, Clement wanted to return to her immediately. His mother and sister stopped this idea. It was too dangerous for him to drive under the circumstances.

They sat and talked. They felt that it was necessary for a mother to have a good recovery period after childbirth. Besides, knowing his wife's expectations of their children, he was certain that she was not able to accept the news.

It was a difficult trial for Clement. He told himself that no more tears were allowed. He had to conceal his sorrow and his knowledge of the problems. He decided to do so, not for himself, but for his wife's sake, for his two older sons' sake, and for the whole family's sake.

He tried his best to show a pleasant face around his wife. Nevertheless, fear haunted him inside. How long could this charade last? Would she find out by observation? What would happen if other people told her?

Clement's world was filled with sadness and the unknown.

SOMETHING IS WRONG

They operated on Randy the third day he was in the Wilmington hospital. Prior to the surgery, Dr. Minor examined the x-ray report. Miraculously, the ending of Randy's colon was further lowered and passed the "marginal point." Therefore, no colostomy was required.

The correction process did, however, require two other procedures. The first step was to free up the membrane in his intestinal area, pull the colon down, create an opening on his bottom, and pull the intestine through the opening. The second step was to trim off the excess piece ten days after the first surgery.

I felt that these ten days were awfully long. I was still weak and trying to recover physically. Clement was exhausted from traveling between Dover and Wilmington.

I was sad but hopeful. I prayed that this would be the only correction required for Randy. At least, he could come home and sleep in the crib I prepared for him. Though I still tired easily, I decided to accompany Clement to the Wilmington Medical Center before the second operation.

To avoid any unexpected surprise, Clement tried to inform and prepare me on the way to the hospital. While he was driving, I recalled the first day of Randy's life. The baby was handed to me in the recovery room. I touched his smooth skin and pinkish face. He was beautiful and appeared to be such a perfect baby. At this moment, I was about to face him again, except this time he would be a child who just went through major surgery and had another operation ahead of him. Joy and sorrow mingled inside me. I was excited but sad. All the way, I thought about his wired and tube-inserted little body. I was afraid. I wanted to hold him, but I was afraid I might hurt him.

Following my husband, I walked through the parking lot and entered the hospital front gate. Clement had become quite familiar with the winding long corridor in the hospital. He had spent many hours in this strange place. We came to the door labeled "IICU." Clement told me it was the Infant Intensive Care Unit, where Randy was.

Clement led me to a decontaminating "scrub" area at the entrance of the IICU. He handed me a blue scrubbing pad, which looked like the one I used in the kitchen, but it was covered with strong, brownish iodine detergent. The pad was a 2" x 3" hard sponge with a piece of brittle plastic brush glued on the back. I scrubbed rigorously under the running water. The smell of the iodine reminded me clearly that this is a serious area in a hospital. I scrubbed hard. The brittle brush made my skin red and hurt my arms and hands. But I wanted to make sure that I was germ-free for my baby's safety. At this moment, a tall person came in, and Clement whispered to me that he was Dr. Minor. He scrubbed himself, too. He scrubbed hard, and it seemed as if he was enjoying it. Clement then introduced me to the doctor. I covered myself with a surgical gown and mask, and Clement did the same thing. We looked at each other. We could see nothing but eyes.

A nurse led me to Randy's incubator. "Randy, Randy," I said, "Mommy is here!" I touched the incubator, still calling to him anxiously but in a low voice.

I looked at him carefully. He appeared to be sleeping

21

peacefully and looked slightly thinner than when he was born. The nurse asked me if I wanted to touch him through the two donut-shaped holes in front of the incubator. I nodded. Cautiously I stretched my hands through the openings. Tenderly I touched him. Tears streamed down my face involuntarily. It seemed as though I was struggling hard to make up for the time we lost in the past nine days. I looked down at my still-extended tummy; I recalled the movement inside me for the past few months. I felt I was very emotionally attached to him before the birth and after the birth. The short hour we spent together before he was taken away from me had intensified my closeness to him.

"Randy, Mommy is here. I am glad that you made it. The first operation is all done. One more, then you will go home. You will see your brothers – Geoffrey and Isaac." I observed every slight movement of his breathing and facial expression while he was sleeping. I did not know how long I had been whispering to him.

"Mrs. Chang, are you all right?" the head nurse asked me.

"I think so. He is so cute!" I replied.

She said, "Yes, he is. Mrs. Chang, would you like to see his incision and the correction Dr. Minor did for him? I am sure that Mr. Chang has explained to you about the two-step procedure. Dr. Minor has completed the first corrective operation. You can see the result, but remember, it is an interim stage. A second surgery is scheduled tomorrow to trim off the excess piece."

"OK, I think I would like to see." I carefully looked at his incision and stitches on his tummy first. It was wider than I thought. It was about four inches across, but long comparing to his tiny body. I ran my finger across my own abdomen and imagined the length proportionally to myself. Dr. Minor had untied Randy's umbilical cord and inserted an intravenous tube into it.

Then the nurse said cautiously, "Mrs. Chang, are you ready to see his bottom?" Her fingers started to peel the tapes on the side of his diaper.

"Yes, I am," I answered

She opened his diaper and showed me the extra piece of colon hanging outside of his body. It looked awkward and painful.

But the second surgery was successfully performed the next day, and a week later Randy was sent home.

At the driveway in front of our house, his grandparents and two older brothers waited for the arrival of our new family member. I knew I was facing a tremendous amount of tasks ahead of me, but I was happy. I had never taken care of anyone who had recently been operated on, but I pumped up every ounce of courage I could at this moment.

We took him into the house and laid him in his crib for the first time. I put my hand on the crib fence and said to myself, "I will do everything and anything I can! This is my commitment."

Randy was weak and pale. He was floppy and without strength. I could not understand why he was so difficult to hold. When I picked him up, I felt that his weight, which was less than seven pounds after the surgery, was like a bag of sand. I put him on my lap and felt as if I was managing a big doll with the weight sinking into me. It was uncomfortable and strange. But I couldn't tell exactly what was so different about this child. I wanted to believe that this was a normal, after-surgery phenomenon.

"Patient caring requires patience," I told myself – patience, patience – other than that, there was nothing I can do.

Randy sucked baby formula from the bottle extremely slow and with no energy. It took up to seven hours a day just to feed him, and I spent another several hours a day in changing his diapers, which could occur as many as twenty times a day. It was a hot summer, and heat rash broke out on him even though we lived in a centrally air-conditioned house. I tried to change the feeding position often. I held him up for a while; I laid him flat on the crib on his back; I tilted him sideways on a small, rolled-up blanket; and often I put him flat on my lap. But whatever way I arranged him, he was difficult to handle.

I could not help but compare him with my first two babies. I searched my memory and recalled the feeling of holding Geoffrey and Isaac when they were infants. Since the first day I brought them home, they had tight muscle tones. They curled themselves up in the fetal position when they slept. I remember how tightly they held their fists. When I laid them down, they rolled up their little bodies like basketballs. This was normal for newborn babies, because this was exactly the position they had in their mother's womb. I remembered when they had sucked their bottles forcefully, and I could hardly pull the rubber nipples out of their mouths. I remembered that I had often quoted the old Chinese saying that describes a person's great effort

24

as being as strong as "the powerful sucking action of infants."

"Where is the powerful sucking action now? How come Randy is not doing it?" I wondered.

Obviously, this common phenomenon did not happen with Randy. He sucked intermittently. His arms, legs, and hands were wide open. His muscle tone was poor. He lay limply on the crib mattress. He reminded me of a frog on the dissecting table in the high-school biology class.

I also noticed that Randy's arms and neck were not strong enough to support the weight of his head. I remember how Geoffrey and Isaac pushed up their heads and looked around with sparkling eyes on the third day of their lives. Even though their eyes were not focused yet for the first few days, they were alert and lively. But with poor Randy, I was even afraid to lay him down on his stomach. I was afraid that he might be suffocated and stop breathing. I moved his head from side to side every so often. I stared at his motionless body, arms, and legs. They sank into the mattress.

For four weeks, I rarely left his bedside. I sat by him. I pulled his crib mattress up to the highest notch to save myself from bending forward all the time. I constantly held a bottle of milk with the nipple in his mouth, waiting for every sucking action from his mouth. I prayed that every drop of the milk would turn into an ounce of energy for Randy's body. Day and night I persisted, and I was exhausted.

Most of the time his eyes were closed. Occasionally he opened his eyes. But his eyesight was dull. I was not sure he could see at all. The progress was snail-like, painfully slow.

When his six-week follow-up was due, I brought Randy to see our children's pediatrician, Dr. Forest, a well-known and respected doctor who was always friendly and caring. He had taken care of Geoffrey and Isaac for the past ten years, and he gave me the feeling that he was always candid and sincere.

For some reason, I felt that Dr. Forest was more reserved this time. Perhaps because of Randy's special physical condition, I realized that Dr. Forest talked to me very tactfully. He examined Randy very carefully. He rubbed his hands on Randy's arms and legs over and over. Finally, softly he told me that Randy's muscle tone was "loose." I asked him whether it was caused by the surgery. He did not answer directly. When I asked again, he answered, "Well, his muscle tone will get better. It is too early to tell at this point. The best thing you can do is just do the best you can." He said a few more encouraging words and brought some hope into my mind.

Two months later I learned that this doctor was instructed by Clement not to tell me about the hidden secret of Randy's condition.

On the way home from the doctor's office, I looked at Randy resting on my arm. I felt pity for him. The operation had taken a toll on him. I couldn't help but question whether this was the normal recovery procedure for any kid who had endured surgery. Didn't a hospital intern tell me that the reason she chose to be a pediatrician was because a child would bounce back from surgery in no time? How come the recovery seemed so slow for Randy? Shouldn't I expect something better? What else could I do?

As I touched his little round face, I did get a little encouragement. I noticed that his face was fuller than a month ago. I looked at his hands and feet. Yes, they were one-third bigger than their size when he first came home. A little voice whispered inside me, saying, "There is hope! This is hope!" Once again I churned up my courage. I believed that I could walk another mile for him.

While I was busy with Randy, Geoffrey and Isaac spent most of the time with each other. They were still happy, nine and ten years old, respectively, except that I noticed that they had become maturer. They tried to be considerate, and they showed their love to their brother regardless of his condition. I would hear them run upstairs and say, "Let's see what Randy is doing." They came to his room and caressed him often. I was thankful and glad to see their expressions of love.

Occasionally I would pick up Randy and walk him from room to room. I talked to him as if he could understand. I told him about his brothers and other family members. I showed him objects in our house, as if he could see. Though his eyes were dim and could only focus on objects for less than a few seconds, I pretended that he was seeing things. I tried to think positively and hopefully.

Nevertheless, hope flows from the strength of the mind, and mental power is connected to physical strength. When the physical strength is gone, the mind surrenders itself to cold reality. Long-term fatigue put my emotional stability to the test. I was very tired. I started to forget what is called "happiness," and I became irritable. Often I lost my temper. I could not recall how to smile. I felt I was no more than a machine, which ran from morning to night and continued from night into dawn. I was depressed and felt skeptical about the situation. One reason I was depressed was because I was being deprived of the minimum rest I needed. I was skeptical because I couldn't figure out the root problem of this child. I wondered if certain truths had been hidden from me. The thought made me nervous and extremely sensitive about other people's reactions toward Randy. A word, a comment, or even a glance from other people could stir up my curiosity and suspicion. I pondered and deliberated on the words of any conversation. My focus was shifted from caring for this child to the reactions of other people. I was burdened not only physically but also mentally. It was like a vicious cycle. My emotions and those of others affected and amplified each other toward the worst dilemma I had ever encountered.

I started to withdraw from people. I questioned people's sincerity when they made any encouraging comments about Randy. I wondered if people were secretly making negative comments about Randy and me. I felt guilty and betrayed. Gradually I became unwilling to handle visitors because my mind wanted to avoid people.

The pain was great. Yet what could I do aside from carrying the burden alone? I did not want to tell anyone, not even Clement.

Hidden tears became part of my life. They dropped on the milk bottle while I was feeding Randy. They dropped on the pillow while I lay down. But I insisted that these tears belonged to me and should not be shared with anyone else.

I spent most of my day in Randy's room. However, my ears had developed a very peculiar and acute sense toward any movement on the stairway. I wanted to make sure to wipe away my tears and relax my face before my two older boys came upstairs. I forced a trace of a smile for them. I wanted to prove that I was a strong person and that I could handle it. As soon as they left the room, my mask fell and usually I wept even more.

I prayed hard. As time went by, even the words of my prayers became frustrated and impatient. I started to complain and be angry about the situation. Rather than asking Gods help, my prayers typically ended with discontentment, argument, and pleading to God: "Lord, why did you give me a child who is so hard to raise? I did not ask for any more babies in my life, and I do not need one more. It was YOU who gave me the third child. Why do YOU put my faith on trial? Lord, it is YOUR responsibility to solve this mess. Oh! My God! I am devastated by the child YOU gave to me. YOU better hurry up and find a solution for me. I just simply cannot go on anymore!"

I tried hard to keep my faith, which at this point was like a lonely boat sailing through a dark, violent sea. Most of the time, it drifted aimlessly. Occasionally I could hear my own helpless groans. The more I looked at Randy, the more questions surfaced in my mind, and the more guilt and discomfort they brought about:

"Something is quite wrong with this child!"

"Why?"

"I don't know, and I don't want other people to know."

"Any answer?"

"I don't know."

I believed that I was the only person in the world who realized the problem of this child. Clement went to work everyday and was busy with his office routine. He always came home with a smile and cheerfully helped care for Randy. From my observation, I was convinced that he did not notice the baby's awkwardness. I told myself that usually men are not as observant about children. Besides it was almost ten years since he handled an infant. I was certain that he would not remember clearly about the muscle tone and strong neck of Geoffrey and Isaac when they were little. Therefore, I decided to keep my doubts to myself.

Day after day the burden became heavier. Sheer fatigue further aggrieved my already saddened heart. Gradually I became more and more negative. I started to question most of the value systems that I had embraced for so many years.

AN UNFORGETTABLE PRAYER

The Annual Family Conference sponsored by the Ambassador for Christ at the Delaware Water Gap was a yearly activity for our family. The conference usually had about four hundred attendees. That year, 1981, was even more special because Clement had been elected chairman of the conference.

During the past year, he had spent much effort to prepare for the conference. He met with the coworkers and the planning committee to prepare the budget, developed programs, and invited speakers. The goal of the conference was to enrich Christian family lives, and it had become an attraction for many families. The size of the conference grew every year, and consequently the resources required for the conference increased.

We had made many friends through the years at this conference. For Geoffrey and Isaac, the conference was the highlight of their year. They enjoyed swimming with their friends and all the activities provided by the children's program. For 1981 our family had more to look forward to. We had anticipated a successful conference, but we were also expecting a healthy baby to be going with us. The baby had been due in June, two months before the conference. Wouldn't it wonderful, we had thought, if we could bring our newborn baby to this conference and share the joy with all our friends? We had considered the timing perfect for us.

However, on June 19, 1981, everything had changed. Randy had been born on that day, and his birth defects had changed our lives and blown away our dream for a wonderful conference. We now faced a dreadful situation with enormous uncertainty. It deprived us of much of the excitement about attending the conference. While the final preparations for the conference were underway, we were spending most of the days dealing with our new ordeal.

Two days prior to the opening of the conference, I was extremely depressed and emotionally inconsolable. Clement felt that I was suffering from fatigue. He told me that he was considering resigning from his chairmanship and canceling the trip.

His idea was quickly opposed by me, his strong-willed wife.

I bluntly said to him, "Oh, no. You can't do that! We can't do that! We must go! You promised a year ago to fulfill this responsibility. Now it is only two days from the conference; you need to be there to complete the work. We must go. The whole family must go, including Randy. I will handle him. I will handle whatever the problems may be." Clement was stunned, but he knew that he could not disregard his wife's determination.

Therefore, we started packing for seven people, including grandparents and three children. We collected playpen, baby formula, diaper, medical supplies, clothes, etc. Before long, our van was full. For sure, we were on our way to the Delaware Water Gap, four hours away from our home.

Conference committee members were waiting when we arrived. Clement set to work immediately.

The conference attendees came from different states on

the East Coast and had a wide spectrum of backgrounds. Some were young couples. Some brought their entire family, including grandparents and young children. Everybody was anxious and was taking this opportunity to have a break from their daily routine.

I got a permission to place Randy's playpen at the back of our main meeting room. The air circulation was great there between two open doors. A washroom in that area was an added convenience. I hoped Randy could sleep well in the mountain breeze.

I fed Randy while I was listening to wonderful speakers. Most of the time he quietly sucked his milk. He slept a lot and seemed comfortable. I managed to handle him from session to session. Probably because my full attention was not solely on him, I felt somewhat relaxed. Amazingly he drank his milk faster and even more during this week. On the third day of the conference, I noticed that his face was fuller than before. His contentment uplifted me. For the first time in three months, I was able to smile truthfully, and I felt hopeful in my heart. Many people gathered around me between sessions. They took turns holding him, caressing him, and walking around with him. They made me feel good.

On the third day of the conference, a lady in her mid thirties came to see me. She asked me if I could remember her.

"I don't think so," I replied. "But, wait a minute, I think I have seen you somewhere. I don't remember your name, but I faintly remember your face."

"Bethel, we both belonged to the Campus Evangelical

Fellowship when we were both students at the National Taiwan University. Remember?" she asked.

"Yes, I recall now. What are you doing here?"

"I was married to a preacher. So I am a preacher's wife. People call me Sister Liu. My husband is the main speaker at this conference – Pastor Liu," she said.

"Oh! I am really sorry for not recognizing you. I should have remembered better," I said.

We reminisced about our old days when we were once young, but they were long gone. I introduced my newborn baby to her. She touched him and commented on his fair complexion. She encouraged me to keep my faith in the Lord. We talked a little more and then went back to our rooms.

A few minutes later, the door to my room was opened. Clement came in and told me that Pastor Liu was on his way to see us. He said that Pastor Liu wanted to pray for Randy.

I was surprised, but I had no objection.

During the past two months, we had received many visits from church friends. Actually sometimes I felt I was overwhelmed, and I really had no more energy to spare. Anyway, most of the time, the visitors carried on the same conversations that I could predict. All of them offered their prayers. Some of them cried with me; some shared Biblical verses; some asked me tons of questions about Randy. Nevertheless, no matter how many visits and sympathizing words I heard, my heart was lonesome.

Pastor Liu came in. He knelt next to Randy, and we all knelt down with him.

He prayed, "Lord, this child is imperfect from a human's standpoint. Yet he was created according to Your perfect plan. You will use him to be part of Your perfect plan. With Your blessing, we will have peace. Amen."

We all cried hard when we prayed. Pastor Liu did, too.

His prayer was short and unique. It was different from any other prayers I had heard. Strangely enough, his prayer was like a seed planted in my mind. The winding road still stretched out ahead of us, but a new seed of hope started to germinate and grow.

Clement left the room with Pastor Liu. Several weeks later, I found that Clement had told Pastor Liu about Randy's congenital problem before the preacher came to see us. Clement had also informed him that the fact was still concealed from me. No wonder Pastor Liu had chosen the words of his prayer very carefully.

Soon I was left alone again with Randy. I looked at the sleepy baby. His eyes, nose, mouth, ears, arms, and legs appeared to be in the right places. I lightly touched his skin and noticed his muscle tone. Once again I felt that he was different, but I could not tell why.

I repeated Pastor Liu's prayer to myself: "This child is *imperfect...* Yet he was created according to Your *perfect* plan."

What did Dr. Liu mean? Why did he say that? I tried to understand, but I got lost in the words. It was like a riddle that I could not solve, or a maze that I could not walk out of. I stared at Randy and thought about Jesus' mother, Mary, who was afraid and puzzled at the moment when she was entrusted with her new responsibility to be a virgin mother. Mary could not understand how it could happen, but she kept the angel's announcement in her heart and pondered over and over. Of course, I could never feel what Mary had felt, but I could not help but ponder the prayer I just heard: Randy is imperfect, but he was created according to Lord's perfect plan.

During the next few days, I was riding on an emotional roller-coaster. I felt that I was being tossed up and down without a defined destination. Deep in my inner chamber there was an unstructured dilemma, full of questions without a single answer. My mind was bewildered by the "imperfect vs. perfect" comparison. I felt that I was like a person entering a combat zone without knowing my allies or my enemies. I was torn and exhausted.

"Oh, Lord, why does my life have to be so confusing?" I cried in my anguish.

Occasionally I found myself holding Randy and saying, "Randy, I am sure you don't understand why you were born into such a mess. Mommy does not understand either!"

This confusion was a part of my very deep pain, a groan that could not be verbally expressed, and my heart suffered in its loneliness.

A GENETIC ERROR?

I sat in the doctor's office waiting for a nurse to call me. It was the second follow-up appointment after Randy's birth. As usual, it was a long wait.

Casually I picked up a *Parents* magazine, opened it arbitrarily, and started to read an article written by a mother. The story described her initial shock and her final victory of accepting her newborn daughter, who was born with "Down's Syndrome," a medical term I had never heard before. The story attracted me, so I continued to read.

"What is Down's Syndrome?" I wondered. I supposed it must be a terrible disease or a set of awful birth defects. What had caused her daughter to be a Down's Syndrome baby? I flipped the magazine back and forth looking for some explanation. The article did mention something about a "chromosome disorder," but it did not give enough details to answer the questions in my mind.

I was amazed by the strong will of the author. She had overcome her disappointment and set her mind to discover the new joy of raising her daughter. Where was her turning point? I was convinced that Down's Syndrome must be a very special medical condition, at least special enough to be in *Parents* magazine.

I finished reading, but my mind was still totally engrossed in the story. Remotely I heard somebody calling my name, but I was not sure where it came from. Suddenly I realized that a nurse was standing in front of me. She said, "Mrs. Chang, please come with me."

I put down the magazine and followed her to get myself

weighed. Then she sent me back to the waiting room and told me to wait again. The previous seat was taken, and another patient was reading the same magazine I had been reading. I found a seat across the room.

I looked at the cover of the magazine from across the room. There was the same mother-and-daughter picture on the front cover as the one inside the magazine. Two columns of facts started to form in my mind. One column was my observations of Randy. The other column was the author's descriptions of her daughter. How similar they were.

This baby girl was born with a heart defect. She was identified as a Down's Syndrome baby immediately after her birth. Her up-slanted eyes and poor muscle tone highlighted the typical traits of a Down's baby. My Randy had defects in his digestive tract instead, and he apparently had not been identified as a Down's Syndrome child. If he were a Down's baby, one of the doctors would have told me by now. Anyway the more I compared the more I found the differences between these two babies.

"Randy is not a Down's Syndrome baby," I told myself. "Don't be so suspicious! There are more differences than similarities. Besides, nobody has mentioned this strange name to me." I felt ridiculous for being so paranoid.

In our conversation that evening, I casually mentioned this article to Clement. I was almost one hundred percent sure that he had never heard of something called "Down's Syndrome."

"Clement, have you ever heard of a medical condition known as Down's Syndrome," I asked.

I was expecting a no for an answer.

"Well, yes, I... did."

I was really surprised. I looked at him and felt that his expression was somehow uneasy and mysterious.

"You did?" I asked suspiciously.

"Yeah.... Well, I think I did..." he answered as if he were avoiding me.

I was puzzled. This was quite different from his normally straightforward personality. I caught a snapshot of his facial expression, and silently I kept my observation inside my heart.

I went upstairs to find an English-Chinese dictionary and a medical dictionary in our study room. I looked up "Down's Syndrome" in the English-Chinese dictionary. Actually I did not expect I could find this medical term in this non-medical book. But I did. I brought it to Clement and said, "Honey, look! It is weird. I don't know why the term 'Down's Syndrome' was translated as 'a Mongolian symptom' in Chinese. Isn't it strange? I bet you have never really heard of something like this before. Have you?" I asked.

"Ah... I did. Mmm... actually, I think I did...." He tried to continue, but he stopped. We were silently looking at each other for a few seconds.

"Clement, this article was quite interesting. It was written by a mother who had a Down's Syndrome baby girl. She said that Down's Syndrome was caused by a chromosome disorder. I don't remember much about biology. Actually I don't think we studied much about chromosomes twenty years ago. Anyway, she said that she

39

was devastated at first, but after a few months of raising her Down's baby, she found that Down's babies are not as bad as most people think they would be. They are not "vegetables." Her daughter not only could make some progress in learning but she is also very cute. This mother finally overcame her sadness and felt the joy of raising her daughter. She accepted the reality and her fate...." I went on and on.

Clement's eyes focused on me and he was concentrating. I was glad he gave me such undivided attention. Abruptly he interrupted me and said, "Can we borrow this magazine from the doctor's office? Do you remember what the cover looks like?"

"I can try tomorrow. It is easy to identify. The picture of the mother and the daughter is right on the cover," I replied. I wondered why he was so interested.

I made a special trip to the doctor's office the next afternoon and asked the staff if I could borrow the magazine for one day, so that I could share an article with my husband. The staff kindly permitted me to do so.

I read the article over again and waited for Clement to come home. I showed it to him as soon as he got home. Surprisingly he said that he had already read it.

"Wait a minute. How can that be?" I wondered aloud.

"Well, I took an hour off from work and drove to the doctor's office to read this special article," he said.

This brought suspicion to my mind, and I wondered silently if this meant that my Randy was a Down's Syndrome child. My heart denied it, but my mind started to be skeptical from that day on. The term "Down's Syndrome" lingered in my brain and occupied my thinking constantly. I launched a secret investigation for myself because I wanted to know more about this medical condition. I found excuses to go to the library. I borrowed books and studied about it.

I learned that Down's Syndrome was indeed caused by a chromosome disorder. Normal chromosomes are arranged in twenty-three pairs – half of every pair comes from each parent. During the cell division, if each chromosome pair does not separate properly, then an abnormal cell results. Medically it is known as "meiotic chromosome non-disjunction." If three sets of genes are formed for the twenty-first pair, a condition known as "Trisomy 21" occurs. Trisomy 21 is the most common reason for Down's Syndrome. It is a natural genetic error and happens randomly. Trisomy 21 is not inheritable from generation to generation. There are two other types of Down's Syndrome cases, namely "Translocation Trisomy" and "Mosaic Trisomy." These two kinds may be inheritable.

This was the first time in my life that I had made up my mind to learn about medical knowledge, and I found it very interesting. I studied hard, and amazingly, not only could I understand them, I gradually remembered those long medical names. I browsed through many chapters when I fed Randy. I studied in the daytime when Clement went to work and hid the books before he returned. For some strange reason, I did not want him to suspect that our baby may be a Down's Syndrome child.

Unfortunately, some of the books I borrowed from the library were written in the 1950s, prior to the modern medical perspectives toward Down's Syndrome children.

41

Since this was my first exposure, I did not know how obsolete these books were. They carried old stereotypes about Down's Syndrome people. Overall the descriptions were negative and pessimistic about their fate. Since they're considered low functioners and many of them were born with some type of internal organ disorder, almost all of them were separated from the mother at birth. They stayed in institutions throughout their short lives. I tried very hard to gain more knowledge about Down's Syndrome, and I felt sorry for them and their parents.

Inside my heart, I firmly disassociated this possibility from Randy. I had seen some improvement with him. Besides, in the past few days, I had noticed that his eyes had started to focus slightly. He had gained some weight and had become stronger. "There is no way for him to be a Down's baby. Our good Lord wouldn't give me one like that!" I assured myself.

While I was enjoying the little improvement, I did notice something unusual. I found that his urination was somewhat intermittent. I was aware of the situation, but I associated this with the scar tissue formed after the surgery. I believed that as time passed, he would get better. I was not too concerned about it.

Every day I worked hard among three children and tried to keep up with my motherhood routine. Fortunately, Geoffrey and Isaac were very considerate and they loved baby Randy very much. I also spent as much time as possible continuing my secret investigation.

IN A DARK NIGHT

I gradually became accustomed to the busy daily routine. I can't say that those days were lively and colorful, but they were manageable. Unfortunately this calm period did not last long. It was only a prelude to the upcoming storm.

One day I noticed that Randy kept his diaper clean longer than usual. At first I was glad, hoping that his bowel control had improved. Then I started to realize that something terrible had happened. Randy had stopped his entire excretory function. For more than ten hours, his diaper was dry. He cried sporadically and his little tummy started to extend. Obviously he was uncomfortable and very tense. He gripped his blanket and pushed against the side of the crib. The situation worsened as hours went by. He screamed with his eyes wide open, and his diaper remained dry.

We called his pediatrician that evening, and the doctor instructed us to give him some laxative and wait for a few hours for the medicine to become effective. We did so. Three hours later, as we hoped and expected, he eliminated a large quantity of stool. He was more relaxed and fell asleep.

Unfortunately, two hours later, his tension returned. I held him on the recliner, rubbed his back, and prayed through the night.

Next morning, I called the doctor again and was informed that he was out of town.

We realized the situation was getting more and more serious. It was twenty-six hours since we first became aware of the problem. His little body continued to become more extended and his tummy swelled to a basketball size. He eyes lost focus and he became less responsive. He was not even crying anymore. His dull eyes seemed to tell me that his little body was giving up!

"Let's take him to another pediatrician. Let's go!" I said. We rushed him to another pediatrician, a partner of Randy's own doctor, and told the receptionist that we must see the doctor right away.

The doctor was stunned at first glance. He touched Randy's tummy and shook his head. Pacing back and forth, he looked confused and nervous. I hoped he would say something but he didn't. Then he left the room to make a few calls. When he returned, he had a small catheter in his hand. He murmured a few words to himself. Then I overheard him said to Clement, "Mr. Chang, I am sure that you know about his *chromosome* situation. Right? And...."

Clement did not answer him, but turned his back toward me. However, I saw their eyes meet; that's when the doctor suspended his sentence abruptly. The doctor instructed me to leave the room so that he could insert the catheter into Randy. Clement stayed in the room to help. I went to the waiting room.

"Didn't I just hear the word 'chromosome'?" I asked myself. "Wasn't it the word I read in the magazine? Does it mean that my Randy is a hopeless kid with the terrible medical condition called Down's Syndrome?" My thoughts were interrupted when I heard Randy's screaming behind the closed door.

Twenty minutes later, the door opened. They came out together, and the doctor handed Randy to me. With a solemn face, he said, "I am going to call the hospital again."

I felt a dark cloud emerge inside me. I looked into my husband's eyes and asked, "Clement, did the doctor mention a word called 'chromosome'?"

"Yes," he answered apprehensively. His facial expression emanated a deep fear.

"What's the matter? What was wrong with Randy's chromosomes? Do you know anything about it?" I pressed my questions.

"Oh, well, he is a little bit different from normal people. He seems… to have some e-x-t-r-a," Clement answered but seemed reserved.

An ominous silence set in between us. A horrific chill crept from my head to my limbs. I tried to keep myself calm, but involuntarily I began to shake.

"He has some e-x-t-r-a. Did you say that? Does the 'e-x-t-r-a' happen on the twenty-first pair of his chromosomes?" I asked.

Completely astonished, Clement was speechless. Finally he said, "YES! But… how do you know all this?"

"Oh, my God! He is a Down's syndrome child! Clement! How come you did not tell me? You mean our baby is a Down's baby? A mentally retarded person? He was exactly what I was afraid of? Oh, no! Oh, my God!"

I was too shocked to cry. I tried hard to keep myself calm, but hatred surged from the bottom of my heart. I felt I was betrayed by my own husband. I was deceived and being kept in the dark. How could my trustworthy husband conceal such important news from me? I was hurt. I felt that I was a fool.

"Clement, how come you did not tell me?"

"I was afraid that you could not take it," he said.

"When did you know?" I asked.

"Three days after he was born," Clement answered.

The doctor returned and said to us, "I have called the hospital. They are expecting Randy. Hurry! Hurry! Don't wait. I really don't know what is going to happen. We just hope for the best. Good luck to you." He talked without much expression. His face told me that the hope was diminishing quickly.

Our local hospital was certainly not properly equipped in the early 1980s. Randy was placed in a regular room with a ten-year-old burn patient. It was awkward to see a tiny baby being placed in the center of a regular hospital bed. The bed was way too large for him. He looked like a baby doll being wrapped in the blanket and thrown to the middle of a large bed. Randy's roommate set the TV to a high volume. It gave me a headache instantly.

An emergency doctor came and gave Randy an enema. They thought Randy's problem was no more than an intestinal blockage. After a catheter was inserted, his tummy was slightly flattened. But to the doctor's surprise, Randy's belly was extended again within an hour. It was unlikely that he could fill up his bladder so quickly. What was actually happening inside him? The doctor did not have a clue. So he decided to transfer him to the Wilmington Medical Center.

We knew that it was getting darker and we wouldn't be

able to return home that night, so we stopped at our house and picked up Geoffrey and Isaac quickly before the transfer.

This was a night of trepidation. Geoffrey and Isaac must have sensed that something terrible had happened, so they sat on the back seat very quietly.

How tragic it was! I was nervous and disappointed. I felt my heart was melting away. I felt that I was deceived by my own husband, a person I always trusted. Worst of all, my fear had become a reality.

I glanced at Clement. He gripped the steering wheel tensely. His expression showed me that he was in great distress.

"Clement, why didn't you tell me?" I asked.

"Bethel, I am sorry. Please forgive me. I had been concerned about this moment of truth. I knew I could not hide the secret from you forever. Many times I tried to come up with the courage to tell you, but I let the day go by because I was afraid to face the consequences. I was concerned that, once I told you, you couldn't take it. Besides, you needed a few days to recover for yourself." He continued, "Bethel, it was very hard for me, too. You know, it was very hard to keep it just to myself and to bear it alone…."

I tried to accept his explanation. "Clement, how could the surgeon determine that he is a Down's Syndrome person?"

"He ordered some genetic test," he replied. Then there was a silence.

It was a rainy night. The road was extremely dark. I began to ask many questions. Every sentence of the conversation chilled both our hearts.

Randy was taken to the Infant Intensive Care Unit again, a place he left merely six weeks ago. We rested the two older boys on a couch in a lounge inside the IICU, and we sat by them. A resident doctor and a nurse prepared Randy for intravenous tubes, monitors, and catheters. I could clearly hear him screaming through the night. His outcry pierced my ears and twisted my heart.

That night, I experienced the worst torture chamber for a mother. That night, I wished the world had come to an end.

LORD! WHERE ARE YOU?

Late that night, Clement and I took the older boys and went to stay at his sister's. I returned to the hospital early the next morning and saw Randy lying in an incubator. His face, strained from crying, was colorless. His head had been shaved and an intravenous needle had been inserted into a vein on the top of his skull, the thin skin of which was covered with at least three dozen purplish needle holes. The skin was raw and bruised. I could not understand why those doctors and nurses could not do a better job of inserting an IV needle. I wondered if they were using Randy as an experiment, which resulted in such an abuse. Randy's mouth was open and obviously he was still crying, but I could not hear any sound from him. He was completely hoarse. His lips were swollen from thirst. I saw his bottom. It was awful. His rectum was pushed out from the pressure, a golf-ball-size mass hanging outside his body. He had no clothes on, not even a blanket. Instead, he was lying under a nest of tubes and wires that interwove across his body. He did not look like the baby I had held only hours ago. As matter of fact, he looked like an electric transformer loaded with circuit lines. His mouth was filmed with dry saliva and the tongue was waxy looking.

I begged the nurses to permit me to soothe his cracked lips with some water or milk. I was given "NO" for answer. No patient was allowed to eat or drink prior to surgery, and besides his organs were not all functioning properly at this point. I asked the nurses if they could tell me about his problem. The answer was simple: "We do not know. The doctor did not tell us." I was frustrated and upset.

My anguish enhanced, I felt nauseated. I thought, "Why? Why? Why does my Randy have to suffer so terribly? Why did he have to be born with such an awful fate? What have I done wrong to deserve this?" I put my arm around the incubator he was in and cried. I felt guilty for bringing him into existence and thus forcing him to suffer in this heartless world.

My mind had lost its ability to negotiate with myself. I had lost my usual calmness. I could not keep my sanity any longer. As I faced this disgusting view of my child, an ineffable hate rose up and occupied my mind. I suddenly felt that the life that I used to have had departed from me. "Normality" was a vague idea that merely existed in the distance. Gradually I became more detached from reality. Everything seemed so remote, including my own family members. Oh, how lonely it was! Nobody, including myself, could understand why my heart was so cold and isolated. Life, to me, was no longer a wide, smooth, and joyful path. Rather, it was a passage inlaid with death and suffering. I felt guilty for bringing such a torturous fate to an innocent child. How could I be so naïve about the cruelty of life? I felt I was thrown into a malicious maze and trapped under an expanding dark cloud. It hovered above me and rapidly lowered to close me in. I was incapable of escaping from it, as if I were a doomed prey frozen still beneath the claw of an approaching predator.

Oh! How much I hated myself. And I hated those people who had lived comfortable lives, because they were spoiled and did not know true suffering.

I hated those people who indulged in their smooth lives and forgot what was called compassion.

I was angered at people who had the luxury of being healthy.

And I was angry with God, because he made Randy and me suffer!

I knew I was losing my mind. My ability to be rational had been stripped away by an irresistible force that had dragged me into a tunnel of despair.

Back at Clement's sister's house, I sat alone motionlessly and gazed about with bewildered eyes. I was still too shocked to cry. My mind was too confused to think. I was on the edge of experiencing a nervous breakdown.

Suddenly I heard Geoffrey and Isaac. They appeared in front of me. Heavily perspiring and breathlessly, they said things such as "Oh my! It is Hot! Hot! Hot! I am so thirsty. Water! Water! Where is water?" Evidently they had been playing outside.

Their requests disturbed me and ignited me with anger for no apparent reason. I denied their requests and howled at them, "Who had told you that you could go outside to play? You are not going to get any water to wet your lips so that you can understand the suffering of your little baby brother. If Randy is not allowed to drink, neither are you!" Then I burst into tears.

My husband and two boys were shocked with what they had heard. They watched me run upstairs, rush into a bedroom, and lock the door behind myself. They heard an ear-piercing scream come through the wall while they tried to push the door open.

Time and space had lost their existence for me. The excruciating pain inside threw me to the floor. I screamed and pounded my head and chest with my fists. I crawled on the floor aimlessly and ripped my blouse. I slammed my head against the wall uncontrollably. Dripping saliva and mucus mixed with tears pasted my face and wet the floor. I heard my own screaming that formed a high-pitched sound and pierced through my eardrums, but I could not stop it. My body rolled all over the floor in a twisted sort of cramping. I felt that my head was bursting, my jaws were coming unhinged, and my heart was shrinking into a tight knot. Half-consciously I knew I should stop the situation, but I couldn't. I had lost control of my mind. I was just like a truck rolling down a hill without brakes.

Finally, when I regained my consciousness, I found I was being held in the arms of Clement. I did not know when had he gotten into the room. My fingers were numb and I could not move my legs. My throat was burning. My tongue was stuck on the roof of my mouth. Clement held me tight, gently rubbed my back, and wet my lips with warm water. He must have held me for quite some time before I started to regain my self-control.

The next day, I looked at myself in a mirror. I was stunned by the image – an ugly, inhuman-looking creature with two goldfish-like swollen eyes. The eyes were bloody red, and the face was covered with thousands of purplish dots. I had bruises all over my body. I suddenly thought about Clement's bloodshot right eye that I saw on the third day after my delivery, when he came to see me at the hospital. Suddenly I understood something. I said to myself,

"Oh, my God! He must have cried his heart out, too."

I felt guiltier now. Not only had I given birth to a defective baby, I had made my husband suffer.

I was devastated and facing a serious mental breakdown. I pictured myself as the "wicked" one, as described in the Book of Psalms, whose life was like chaff being blown away by the wind. Hope started to fade from my heart. Illusions, mixed with hatred, disappointment, helplessness, and lamentations, occupied me. I hallucinated about terrible images that did not exist.

I was like a doomed fruit fly, being caught and pinned on the wall, waiting to die, but I could not die easily.

LET GO?

The x-ray showed that there was something like a big water balloon inside my Randy's abdomen. It was an extraordinary medical phenomenon. The doctor called it a "medical wonder," because it was a good case for medical students to learn about.

The "balloon" was actually an abnormal development of the missing colon at the lower end of Randy's digestive system. This missing piece had "relocated" to form an enclosed cavity and had embedded itself inside the abdominal membrane. According to the doctor, the cavity originally had been small, empty, and probably quite dry at birth. But since the wall of the cavity had the structure of intestinal lining, at some point it had started to produce mucus. Gradually this cavity became filled up with sticky fluid and started to expand. It inflated rapidly and jeopardized the normal functioning of the neighboring organs. The weight of this "water balloon" increased and pressurized the other organs. It collapsed the passage of his urinary tract and stopped the flow of urine. It blocked the intestine and formed a bottleneck in the digestive tract. The mucus-filled cavity continued to expand and threatened other important organs. Finally, Randy's body inflated terribly.

The cavity was not a tumor. It was actually a hole similar to a tooth cavity. Since it was not a mass, it could not be cut out and removed. The doctor told us that the only way to solve the problem was to chemically destroy it from the inside.

"But how?" I asked the doctor.

"Frankly, I don't know yet. Nobody has done anything like this," he answered.

The fluid continued to accumulate. The condition was critical. The cavity became a time bomb inside Randy's body. His life was threatened.

In order to relieve the pressure, the doctor followed the x-ray map and inserted a needle into Randy's tummy to extract some fluid from the cavity. It worked for a while, and then the fluid built up again.

Finally, the doctor laid out his strategy for solving the problem. As a result, Randy underwent four major surgeries within one month, and every step was risky. The first step was to create a drainage system. The doctor made an incision on Randy's lower back and inserted a tube to relieve the internal pressure. A few days later, the doctor made a vertical incision on Randy's tummy and tried to expose the cavity. Unfortunately, after the doctor had made a long opening, he found that the cavity was actually hiding behind several major organs. He could see it but was not able to reach there without hurting other organs. Without a choice, he closed the incision and sent Randy back to his room. He consulted other doctors at the Johns Hopkins Hospital and Boston Children's Hospital, for help. Ten days later, he decided to do surgery on Randy's body from the back again. This time he made another incision, and finally he reached the cavity. He cleaned up the cavity wall and coated it with a strong acid. His goal was to destroy the wall and stop it from producing more mucus.

During this month, my heart ached for Randy. Could

anybody imagine the pain he had to endure? He went through four major surgeries in a ten-day interval. His intestines had to be burned by the chemical acid. I remembered how painful it was when I had accidentally touched a drop of strong acid in my chemistry lab when I was in high school. How could he tolerate that? When the pain from one surgery was barely subsiding, he was taken in for another surgery. He cried, but nobody could help. If he could have verbalized his feelings, he may well have said that his tummy was experiencing something like World War III.

For medical students, Randy was certainly a medical wonder. Since Wilmington Medical Center was a teaching hospital, Randy's case provided an extraordinary opportunity for medical studies. Though I believe in education, I was annoyed by their excessive observation. They treated my Randy as a valuable patient who must be studied by all interns and residents. Everyday Randy was visited by teams of medical students. They looked at him and flipped him back and forth at their convenience. They discussed their findings while he was crying. They changed his intravenous needle from his umbilical cord to his already-bruised small hands, then to his foot, then to his head. They shaved part of his new-grown hair everyday so that they could change the needle from one vein to another. Oh, what a pitiful head it was! It looked like a needle cushion made from a purplish fabric.

I was outraged. I could not stand the torturing of Randy by those inexperienced medical interns and resident doctors anymore. I wished I could argue with them and tell them that they were inhumane and incompetent. But I had to restrain myself out of fear that they would abuse my Randy even more. After all, Randy was only their patient, not their child. Besides, no matter what mistakes they made, Randy would not be able to communicate verbally, and he would be compliant.

Randy's tummy looked awful. A hole had been made in his lower abdomen and bladder to secure a catheter for his urination. He was surrounded by a mass of tubes, bags, and machines. Once again, Randy did not look like a normal human baby anymore.

Every surgical procedure brought us hope, and was followed by a profound disappointment. The frequent surgeries within such a short period of time caused me to suffer an almost unbearable psychological depression.

The situation worsened. One day, a doctor came to me and said, "Mrs. Chang, I have to tell you something realistic. Randy's long-term prognosis is not good. His medical complication has put him in a very difficult situation. Even though we think we have destroyed the lining in his cavity, we cannot guarantee that his urinary function will resume. The prolonged usage of a catheter may have disabled the normal function of his muscle control for urination. If his urination ability was lost, then he may get urinary poison, and his life will be threatened immediately."

He paused for a moment, then he continued, "Mrs. Chang, you are in a very difficult situation. Say if Randy miraculously survives this situation and resumes his urinary function, then he will go home with you. But then you know you will be facing a formidable challenge for the years

57

to come. It is a tough life for you and your family." He stopped and looked at me.

"What do you mean?" I asked.

"You will be labored for your entire life, Mrs. Chang. Most likely he is going to be a low functioner. It is probable that he will not be able to control his bowels and urinary tract. He may not be able to walk and talk normally. This is going to be long-term suffering. It will exhaust you and make your life very difficult! Oh! There is another thing. Generally speaking, a Down's Syndrome person's life expectancy is much shorter than normal people's. So, he may only live to twenty years old." The doctor patted my back. "Well, Mrs. Chang, take it easy. Remember: God gives! God takes!" He left the room.

Facing the helpless baby once again, I felt an excruciating pain. Sadness took control of me. Suddenly the volcano inside me erupted. A river of tears roared down my face. My legs lost strength and I could not balance myself. I was overrun by my grief.

Clement hauled me outside. We stumbled through a crowd of people and made our way through the parking lot. I cried aloud as I walked, "Randy! Oh! Randy! I don't think you are going home with us anymore! R-a-n-d-y! If you are going to die, please go quickly. Otherwise, you will have to suffer longer. Your life is too hard for you. Please do not drag it on. P-l-e-a-s-e...."

Suddenly, I realized that I was a few steps away from a tombstone. How come I had never realized that there was a graveyard right next to the parking lot and almost adjacent to the hospital? What a weird scene in the city! Why would

58

those people want to be buried right outside the hospital? Or the hospital was built right next to the cemetery? Was that an ominous sign? Never in my life had I had such a strange feeling of the closeness of life and death. Actually they are only a breath away.

Clement led me to the car. He drove us back to our home in Dover. I cried all the way. He held my hand but could not utter a word of comfort. He did not cry, but I know his heart did.

Clement parked his car in front of a restaurant after we returned to Dover.

"Honey, let us go in and eat something before we go home. Ok? You need to calm down!" he said.

It was 9:00 p.m., almost closing time. There were only two people talking at a table near the center of the restaurant. I was glad that it was almost empty. I was not in any condition to meet any acquaintances. I walked toward the back corner.

I passed by those two people quietly. The light was dim, and I could not see their faces.

I pulled out a chair and was ready to sit down.

"Bethel, is it you?" one of the two people called out to me.

I was surprised and somewhat irritated. What luck to meet somebody I know at this hour under this condition!

"Yes! Who are you?" I asked.

Clement said, "Oh! Hi, Gloria! When did you come back?" He walked over to greet her and her husband.

Mr. and Mrs. Smith had been fellow church members before. They had moved away two years ago, and we did not expect to see them in town.

Gloria was a very special lady in our church. Occasionally she would be filled by the Holy Spirit and speak in tongues. She sang in the choir. Her sparkling eyes, energetic voice, and wide smile brought a strong spiritual sense to the congregation. She looked happy all the time. We missed her since they moved away.

She asked me about my children. I told her briefly about Randy's condition.

Gloria told me that her father just passed away two days ago. They came home to attend his funeral. She told me that it was very difficult for her to lose her father. For several days she found it almost impossible to accept the fact. Finally, she submitted herself to God's will and simply "let go" in her mind. Then, interestingly, she felt peace and joy return to her heart.

"Bethel, God has His own time for everything. Try to lean on this principle. I am sure peace will return to you," she said.

I tried to eat, but the food was tasteless. I felt lousy and could not get over the death of Gloria's father. "Misery loves company!" I said to myself, "I just cannot get away from death, even in a restaurant."

I was tired, but I could not sleep. I was exhausted the next day. I went into Randy's room, sat alone, heavy hearted, and recalled what had happened the day before.

"Let go! Let go!" I seemed to hear Gloria telling me.

"Can I?" I asked myself.

"No, I cannot!" I said to myself.

"God has His own time for everything…." Gloria's

words emerged in my mind again.

"Then, why, Lord? Why did You send Randy to me for nothing but pain and suffering? Oh! God! You are not fair," I said silently.

A big knot formed inside my heart. It burdened me and dragged me down deeply into a trench. Angrily I cried out loud to God, "You are not fair! You are not fair! I cannot tolerate the suffering you gave me anymore."

I secluded myself in an emotional torture chamber during the next two months. I could not face Randy's room at home. His empty crib amplified my sadness. So I locked up his room. I could not receive any guests and friends who came to see me. Whatever they said added extra burdens to me. Hallucinations possessed me during the day, and frightening nightmares haunted me in the night. My mind was forced to enter into a strange land where I was chased by scary dreams and horrible images. Sometimes I could not distinguish facts from imagination. Every time we drove by a cemetery, I could vividly see a tombstone with Randy's name carved on it. It was an illusion, of course, but it looked so real. I was terrifying myself. I tried hard to pull myself back to reality, but my rationality was too weak to combat the shadows that haunted me.

Gradually I became more distant from people. Though I still had a few trustful friends, most of the phone calls and uninvited visitors were irritating to me. One day, a social worker came to see me. She told me I could institutionalize Randy if I felt that I could not handle him in the future. I told her, "No, thanks." Friends could be opinionated, but I was convinced that they did not really understand my problems. I was troubled by some people who erroneously blamed me for taking birth control pills that may have caused the baby's abnormality. Essentially, tactlessly, they were telling me that I was responsible for Randy's birth defect. However, I found that I could not defend myself under their presumptions.

I found myself in a predicament similar to Job's situation in the Old Testament. Job suffered alone and was advised by several opinionated friends. God allowed Satan to attack Job because He wanted to prove to Satan that Job could retain his steadfast faith to God even under the stress of calamities. Job did. Later, God blessed him in many ways.

But I was not Job, and I didn't have the same level of faith. I should not have been picked as a victim.

I was very angry at my fate. So I decided to have a final showdown with God.

On a piece of paper, I wrote down my arguments. With a hysterical cry and my fist hitting the floor, I read them aloud, and demanded that God give me answers.

"Are you a true living God?" I shouted. "Why are you so unfair as to make me suffer so horribly? I feel angry about the fate you gave me. What should I do? What are you going to do to me next? If you are a true living God, then, stretch out your arms and solve my problems now. You have ruined my life, caused me to lose my will. Now I don't have any strength left to continue my narrow path!

"I am not going to struggle to show people that I am a Christian anymore, because I have sacrificed too much," I continued. "If you are a true God, then prove it to me and do something good for me!"

I read it over and over. My voice was louder and louder. I was enraged. I was like a child kicking and throwing things. I felt as if I were the prodigal son ready to betray my Father and leave home.

"Let go!" Gloria's voice came to my mind.

The voice entangled itself with my own denial.

"No, I can't! I can't! I have suffered enough. I am tired of the hypocritical mask worn by many Christians! I have experienced a horribly painful fate. Oh, Lord, I am sorry. I am really sorry. But I will let YOU go!" I ranted like a rebellious child getting ready to abandon her nest.

I decided not to pretend anymore. I wanted to be honest about my feelings.

So I said to God, "I am sorry, God! I am leaving you. Goodbye!"

FIRST LIGHT IN THE DAWN

A popular song was being broadcast by a local Christian radio station quite often. It came to my ears almost every time I traveled between Dover and Wilmington. At first I couldn't quite discern the words. However, the beautiful melody attracted me to listen carefully and learn the words. I began to sing along with the refrain:

> "Because He lives, I can face tomorrow.
> Because He lives, all fear is gone.
> Because I know He holds the future,
> And life is worth the living just because He lives."

Deep down in my heart I was resisting every line the hymn was saying. Is God really living? This was my big hang-up. Could a living and loving God allow the difficulties that I encountered? Sure, I was reminded of the familiar Biblical story of Job and his suffering. But I am not Job, so why should God use me to show off His power against Satan? Why was my son caught in the crossfire? My heart was filled with bitterness and anger. "It's just not fair!" I repeated to myself.

My antagonism against God compounded the anguish inside me. Now I not only had to face a seriously handicapped son but also my own wounded heart. The scar seemed to challenge what I had believed all along.

Nevertheless, the enticing melody and soothing words of this hymn continued to flood my ears as soon as I got in the car.

"God sent His son. They called Him Jesus.
He came to love, heal and forgive;
He lived and died to buy my pardon.
An empty grave is there to prove my Savior lives.

How sweet to hold our newborn baby,
And feel the pride and joy he gives;
But greater still the calm assurance:
This child can face uncertain days because He lives.

And then one day, I'll cross the river.
I'll fight life's final war with pain;
And then death gives way to victory.
I'll see the lights of glory and I'll know He reigns.

Because He lives, I can face tomorrow,
Because He lives, all fear is gone.
Because I know He holds the future,
And life is worth the living just because He lives."

I didn't know the background of the composer or when the song was composed. Why would the composer's "holding a newborn baby" be much different from mine?

One quiet afternoon, I looked up the words of this hymn from a songbook that I bought at the Christian Family Conference. I sat alone and tried to sing it softly, meditating on the words. Tears burst in my eyes while a tiny voice magnified itself inside me saying: "I will strengthen you and make you strong!"

The last sentence of the refrain says, "Life is worth the living…." I began to wonder, is life really worth the living? To someone in my situation? As sad as little Randy? If life is worth the living for all people throughout the ages, it must also include the life of Randy. *Then the value of life is not merely measured by its span but by the union of the life and the Life-giver.*

After days of doubt and rebellion, I faced a final decision. Could I completely overturn what I had believed in? I couldn't deny the existence of the Creator, nor could I bid farewell to the root of life. If I accepted what I had believed in, then I had to acknowledge the value of life, destined by the Life-giver, and live it out without any complaints. But it's so much easier said than done. I was really caught in a dilemma.

What should I do?

I glanced through the words of the hymn again: "This child can face uncertain days because He lives." Is "facing uncertain days" really the life that is worth Randy's living?

Pastor Liu's prayer several months back in the Summer Family Conference rang in my head again: "Lord, we often cannot understand what You have prepared for us. Randy is an imperfect child from a human's standpoint. Yet, he was created according to Your perfect plan. I firmly believe You will use him to be a part of Your perfect plan."

I heard a voice closing in on me: "Are you still fighting and denying everything? It's time to make your decision. Do you want to leave God or accept the challenge of life?" There was another tiny voice I had heard before, saying: "He will strengthen you and make you strong. Why not

66

learn to trust Him? It's much easier to trust the Lord than to resist Him. Those trusting the Lord don't have to find excuses to resist Him."

While I was still hesitating in that miserable night, Gloria Smith's advice flashed back in my mind: "Let go! God has His own time for everything...."

My heart was eventually softened. Tears broke through like a roaring river, and I responded to God: "OK. I'll let go!" Once again I sang the refrain of the favorite hymn: "Because He lives, I can face tomorrow. Because He lives, all fear is gone. Because I know He holds the future, and life is worth the living just because He lives."

Every sentence and each word in this hymn now reflected the new hope in my heart. It was like a feast in a gloomy valley of death. I was thankful that the Lord had spoken to me through various people at different times and places. Their words were like seeds sown in my heart. They grew and flourished and became my strength and comfort in times of need. Yes, the Lord would renew my strength as He had repeatedly promised.

At that moment, I was like the prodigal son in the Biblical parable, welcomed by the tender loving Father, who stretched out his arms holding me tightly to himself. The melody "The Lord Is My Everlasting Arm" rang through my ears, reminding me that "I HAVE COME HOME!" I wanted to return to the roots of my faith, asking my Heavenly Father for the healing of my son and praying for the daily strength I needed to move on. A ray of life and hope grew stronger and brighter inside my once-darkened heart.

With a Bible in my hands, I asked God, "Lord! What kind of people did you heal when you were on earth? Did you heal all who asked you to?" I combed through the four Gospels searching for clues and finally shaped an answer. Now I understand! Our Lord Jesus did heal all who truly believed in Him and asked Him for healing. He healed everyone who came to Him and never refused anyone. I was very thankful for His amazing, loving kindness toward those who sought Him.

In the evening, my friend Kelly called to find out how Randy was doing. She also told me her own experience – praying for the healing of her eldest child. She asked me: "Do you know what was the most intriguing thing in this episode?" Holding my breath, I was waiting for the answer. She then said: "I discovered that in Jesus' days He never turned away anyone who sought His healing."

My hands were trembling. Suddenly I realized how Peter, the apostle, felt at the moment he recognized the Lord, who told him to cast the net on the right side of the boat for fish. I was literally shaken because He had sent a messenger to proclaim His truth and faithfulness just at the time I needed assurance!

A few days later I received a booklet entitled "Healing – For Your Loved One and Yourself" from a sister in our church. I knew, beyond any doubt, that this wasn't accidental. God wanted to speak to me through the author.

I carried this booklet in my purse, studied the contents, and memorized as many of the cited Bible verses as I could, hoping to find out the true meaning of "healing." I asked God bluntly: "The people you have healed in the past have all died physically. Why did you bother to heal their temporary lives? You are a great physician and the Creator, and you promise to open the door when someone knocks, and to be found for those who seek you. Lord, I pray that you will give me the answer."

Little Randy was still in the hospital. His complex medical problems kept the doctors and the medical team quite busy. His case had been sent to the Johns Hopkins Hospital for evaluation and review by specialists because it was unique. He was still surrounded by interns and residents who wanted to examine him and learn something about his situation. We continued to feel sorry for Randy, having to put up with all this.

In a special meeting at church, the main message was "God's Healing." After that, I learned to commit and entrust little Randy into the hands of the Creator and diligently to seek the reality of God's healing.

Gradually I came to a better understanding of the essence of this healing. God is the Creator, who has the power to create and to re-create. He can create human beings with different physical conditions and personalities, and He also has the power to change them. The motivation for creation and re-creation is not for the good of those created but for His own glory. God's healing is His promised gift to humankind because He loves everyone in this world. God's healing is defined in His eternal plan, often beyond human comprehension. A human being is composed of body, mind, and spirit. God can heal someone's physical ailments, relieve his pains, and extend his life to some extent, but the body will eventually die. Only healing of the spirit can and will last into eternity, and this is the greatest gift from God to man.

Although my heart still ached for my child, my inner strength grew stronger with time. Even though I was emotionally frail and physically tired and worn out, I was no longer struggling, nor trying to find reasons to be rebellious. I tried to pray as consistently as I could. Every morning I asked God for sufficient strength to complete the tasks laid before me for the day. At night I would kneel by my bed and thank Him for His sustaining grace. During my busy schedule, I could still find time to meditate on the scripture verses cited in the booklet "Healing – For Your Loved One and Yourself." On the road to and from the hospital, my husband and I would sing the hymn "Because He Lives" over and over again. Yes, I said to God, just like the hymn says:

> "This child can face uncertain days because He lives....
> Life is worth the living just because He lives....
> Because He lives, I can face tomorrow."

AN IMPERFECT PERFECTION

"Shirley is in the hospital, again!" my friend told me on phone.

"Which hospital?" I asked.

"Well, her situation is getting worse. The local hospital did not keep her. She has been transferred to the Wilmington Medical Center, where Randy is," she said.

Shirley, a friend of mine, was a lovely Chinese lady in her early forties. She had been taken to the emergency room a year before, following a sudden stomach pain. A biopsy revealed tragic news: she had cancer. Surgeons later removed her whole stomach and replaced it with a section of her large intestine. She had a very difficult time after the surgery. She told me that she was haunted by a multitude of evil spirits every night. She was terrified by their presence every time she closed her eyes. They accused her and threatened her. After she was released from the hospital, she underwent many months of chemotherapy. Her body reacted violently to the medication. It was unbearable for her to feel nauseated all the time. Finally, she decided to give up the chemotherapy.

At first, Shirley felt better. As matter of fact, she felt so wonderful that she was able to drive around. Nevertheless, the happiness did not last long. The cancer spread rapidly in her body. Suddenly, one day her sharp pain returned, and she was sent to the emergency room. The prognosis was bad. The doctor declared that her case was "final".

Shirley was taken to the Wilmington Medical Center Cancer Unit, only five minutes away from where Randy was. We decided to see her every other day after we visited Randy.

One evening, after visiting Shirley, Clement said to me, "Bethel, I believe that the Lord wants us to share the salvation of Jesus Christ with Shirley. He has entrusted us with this responsibility. What do you think?"

I agreed, but I did not know how to pursue it.

That night, I knelt down and opened my heart: "Lord, you sent me to Shirley. I don't even know where to start. My ability is limited. I need advice from you so that I know that you are with me. Lord, you gave Elijah advice when he faced a challenge on Mt. Carmel against Baal's prophet. So, I ask you to show me your presence and give me the courage for my mission. I need your wisdom and a clear direction. I know I cannot fight this spiritual war with my own strength. So, Lord, help me."

I specifically also asked the Lord to give me some assurance about Randy's future. I wanted to know that Randy's soul was saved no matter how long he would live. Two scripture verses came to my heart before I went to bed:

> Jesus said, "I praise you, Father, Lord of heaven and earth, because you have hidden these things from the wise and learned, and revealed them to the little children" (Matthew 11:25).

> "In the same way, the Spirit helps us in our weakness. We do not know what we ought to pray, but the Spirit himself intercedes for us with groans that words cannot express. And he who searches our hearts knows

the mind of the Spirit, because the Spirit intercedes for the saints in accordance with God's will." (Romans 8:26-27)

My heart was comforted. I suddenly understood the great power of the Holy Spirit. Even though I could not communicate with Randy verbally at this moment, the Holy Spirit certainly could communicate with him in a different dimension. When human understanding seemed to cease, the Holy Spirit's work continued. It could easily teach Randy in its own way. My heart should not be worried.

We continued to visit Shirley. She always greeted us with a lovely smile. Shirley was definitely one of the best patients. She was a cheerful character. Even in the final stages of cancer, she tried to keep a smile on her face. Nurses commended her as being the most pleasant patient. Occasionally, she groaned and mourned when the pain from the cancer overpowered her. Aside from that, she kept her sense of humor and had a positive attitude. She even told me that she would like to start a small business if she could recover from cancer. She also said that she wanted to go to church with me someday.

After many visits, Shirley and I became much closer. She started to unveil her deep sorrow inside. One day she said to me, "Bethel, I am really scared. My roommate passed away last night. They pushed her away. I was very uneasy throughout the night. Bethel, someday, they will push me out of this room, too. I will no longer be here. I am so helpless and sad." I noticed the tears in her eyes. She looked very depressed.

My heart trembled. "Oh! My Lord! My God! What should I do now? Please give me the words of wisdom. Help me so I can help Shirley!"

I sat by Shirley, wiped her tears, and said to her, "Shirley, many thoughts have gone through my mind lately. I am sure you have thought of a lot of things, too. We both are experiencing a tough situation in our lives. In my case, Randy's survival is still an unknown. For the past few months, I went through a big battle inside. I was depressed and angry. I hated myself. I hated God for being unfair to me. I was torn inside out. To tell you the truth, I almost had a nervous breakdown. Day and night, I was haunted by the illusions. But, Shirley, you know, I wrestled with God, and I did not win. The Lord won and brought me back to His side. He changed me and gave me new hope. I have learned to view life from a different perspective now. Would you like me to tell you what I have found?"

"Yes, I'd like to hear it," Shirley answered.

With her consent, I tried to explain. "Shirley, I believe in the existence of a living God. I believe that everybody has a soul. God is immortal. He lives from eternity to eternity. Because of his creation, all things follow orders. Each of our lives is merely a small fraction of the lives in the whole universe, across an infinite time span. Life is a gift from God. But human beings are special because we were created according to God's image. Each one of us has a soul. We belong to both mortal and immortal cycles of lives. Our earthly lives are mortal, but our souls can be immortal. Our earthly life could not alone give us our inheritance of the full value of eternity. But God gave us an

74

opportunity to be transformed and become more valuable."

I paused and looked at Shirley. She signaled me to continue.

"Shirley, there is one thing no one can escape. Everybody will finish earthly life sooner or later. Some people live long lives, maybe seventy, eighty, or even over one hundred years old. Some live short lives. Some babies may only live for a few days. The oldest person in the Bible was Methuselah. He lived 969 years. But then, what happened to him, Shirley? He died. Do you realize that, Shirley? They all died. Even those people who were healed by Jesus eventually died. The mortality rate of human beings is 100%. Then, what is the value of 'life'? I believe the value of life comes from connecting ourselves to the root of life. God is the origin of life. He is the root. The longevity of human lives is tiny compared with the infinite scope of eternity. A few decades or a few centuries are all so insignificant. Shirley, do you agree?"

"Interesting point! But why do you think the value of life comes from connecting ourselves to the root of life?" Shirley asked.

An analogy came to my mind. "Shirley, look, how is a pair of gloves made? Aren't they created according to the image of our hands?" I asked.

"Sure they are," she replied.

"Do gloves have any value when they just lie around? Of course not. But once you wear them, the gloves become valuable. Why, because they were connected to the 'root' of the image," I said.

"Good thinking. It really makes sense," Shirley said.

Light Into Dawn – Randy's Miracle

I continued, "Now, let's talk about Randy. His prognosis is really uncertain at this point. His life may only last for a few months. But even so, his life is valuable. The value is measured by a yardstick provided by the Creator according to His own value system. Shirley, I could not fully understand God's value system. But I believe in this value system. Therefore, my life is valuable and so is yours."

"How could a person make his or her days more valuable?" she asked.

"I believe that a 'valuable day' is a day we spend in such a way that is in concert with God's will and pleases Him. In contrast, for those days that we spend in disconcert with God's will, these days are invaluable and wasted. Therefore, a person who lives a longer physical life may not have more valuable days than the ones who have a shorter life. One day we will face our Creator, and He will show us the counting of our days."

Shirley was totally engrossed in my talking. I touched her hand and continued. "Shirley, I really had been thinking deeply in the past two months, but I was sure of one thing. I know that Jesus loves me, and He lives. Faith cannot be delivered in a halfway skeptical manner. The power of the faith is given to a person who believes in God's word heartily. The Bible told us that Jesus was given birth by the Virgin Mary. He redeemed me and saved my soul through his own crucifixion and resurrection. Shirley, I know that sometimes you feel lonely. Why don't you spend sometime thinking about this spiritual domain? Maybe you will understand what I am saying."

I surprised myself with all the words I had said. I felt as

if I was actually talking to my own heart and from my heart. I felt calm, sincere, and peaceful inside.

Shirley broke her silence and said, "You know, Bethel, if anyone had told me that Jesus is still loving me, I would have questioned it. They do not and cannot understand my inner pain. Those people live healthily and happily. Of course, they have all the reasons to thank God. But, I am not that lucky. I am still young, but I am sick and dying. My body is giving up on me. I only have a limited number of days left in this world. How can I say that God cares for me? You and Clement are so special to me. When nobody else comes to see me, you do. Your situation is not easy either. Randy's prognosis remains unknown and difficult. You are experiencing a very difficult time in your life. I am sure you have thought a lot. You have sought answers for yourselves. With all the struggles, you drew a conclusion that Jesus still loves you. You're convinced that life has its value. You believe that there is a life after the earthly life. Maybe you are right. Maybe I should think about it, too."

So, I asked Shirley to pray with me. She did.

As Clement and I drove home, I thought about Shirley and Randy. I tried to count how many times we had traveled between Dover and Wilmington. We did not know how exactly we had gone through our days, but I learned not to burden myself with tomorrow. Actually, I really did not have the energy to worry about tomorrow. The burden from today was sufficient for me to bear. I prayed for Shirley's salvation. I asked God to give the doctors wisdom to solve my Randy's cavity problem in his tummy. I also thanked God for giving me the opportunity to share the good news of Jesus' salvation with Shirley.

That evening, for a strange reason, Clement and I felt uneasy at home. It was late, but we had an urge to talk to Shirley. So we called her around ten o'clock.

Shirley was so happy to hear from us. Actually, she was anxious to talk us, too. She told me that since we had left earlier that afternoon, a new thought occupied her mind. It excited her and kept her awake. She tried to pray, and she asked God to reveal to her heart the mystery of life. Her heart was touched by the love of God. She suddenly realized how much the Creator of the universe had loved her. Therefore, she made an important decision. She decided to accept Jesus Christ as her personal savior. That night, Shirley made the most important choice in her life. Over the phone, she asked me to make an arrangement for her baptism on the hospital bed.

In the next few days, Clement and I spent much time talking to Shirley. We witnessed her baptism. It was an experience we would always remember. We saw the happiness radiating from the face of a dying cancer patient. A firm assurance flew into her heart. Tears of joy flowed down her cheeks to her chin. She held my hand and said repeatedly, "Oh! I am so happy! I am so happy! I am saved. From now on, I belong to the kingdom of God...." We all forgot the physical pain and the worries that had troubled us. We were overwhelmed by the joy and thanksgiving there in her room.

Shirley's health declined rapidly. Before she entered into a complete coma, she woke up occasionally. She was calm and peaceful. Every time she was awake, she requested other people to pray with her. The fear of death could overpower her no more. A few days later, she completed her earthly journey and started a new phase of her life, a life in eternity.

Through this experience, Pastor Liu's prayer became clearer and more meaningful to me. God can use a seemingly imperfect person to complete His perfect plan.

While we were busy with Shirley, miraculously, Randy's condition started to improve. He became more responsive, and his milk intake increased. He was definitely getting better, but the doctor was very concerned about Randy's urination. He had depended on the bladder catheter for more than two months. It was questionable whether his normal urination could resume. It was highly likely that the muscle had lost its ability to perform the normal control. After the doctor removed his catheter, everybody waited nervously. We prayed for hours. Nurses checked his diaper frequently. Two hours later, the IICU burst out in cheers. A nurse shouted excitedly, "Randy has wet his diaper!" Everybody came to kiss Randy. It was wonderful to know that Randy's urinary tract had started to function normally again.

In the past few months, Randy had endured immense pain and suffering physically. Several different times, a surgeon's scalpel had penetrated his little body in different parts. He had been admitted to the hospital on a hot summer day, and discharged two days before Thanksgiving. Despite all the odds, his cognitive ability started to improve. He started to respond to my cooing. At five months of age, he started to smile. He ate more and was about to sleep overnight.

Light Into Dawn – Randy's Miracle

On the homecoming day, I chose a new baby sleeper from a pile of gifts that I had received several months ago in a baby shower. I realized many of them had become too small for him. Randy had been wearing a hospital gown for the past two and half months.

Nurse Rose, who had spent most of her shifts caring for Randy, prepared him for discharge. She took off Randy's "hospital uniform" and gave him a new look in the new sleeper. Everybody in IICU came to see the "real" baby Randy. Rose had become quite attached to Randy, but she was really happy to see him going home. She combed Randy's new-grown hair and kissed him again and again. She held Randy all the way to our car. With tears, Rose gave him the last kiss before she handed him to me.

In the midst of joy, the doctor's warning still rang in my ears: "Mrs. Chang, I have to tell you the truth about the prognosis of this child… Even though a miracle may happen… you will be facing a formidable challenge… You will be labored for your entire life, Mrs. Chang. Most likely, he is going to be a low functioner. He will not be able to control his bowels and urinary tract. He may not be able to walk and talk. This is going to be a long-term suffering. It will exhaust you and make your life very difficult!"

"Oh! My Lord, Help me, please! I know the road ahead is not easy," I thought. "Give me the strength I need, please!"

The melody of the song "Because He Lives" surfaced in my heart, and I started to sing:

"How sweet to hold our newborn baby,
And feel the pride and joy He gives.
But greater still the calm assurance:

This child can face uncertain days because He lives.

"Because He lives, I can face tomorrow.
Because He lives, all fear is gone.
Because I know He holds the future,
And life is worth the living just because He lives."

"Randy, my little sweetheart! I know you have gone through a lot in the past two months. So did your daddy and mommy. Together, we have walked through a very unusual path of life. Mommy loves you. We will start all over again and do it together," I said softly to Randy when Clement drove up our driveway.

Grandpa, Grandma, Geoffrey, and Isaac had waited a long time in front of our house. Our home, through the turmoil, was united again. Our family, together, was ready to face the new formidable challenge that lay ahead of us.

For this day, we rejoiced. We praised God for his mercy and the gift of "re-creation."

Yes, it was sweet to hold our newborn baby.

Yes, we felt the pride and the joy God had given us.

In our household, we offered our deepest and most sincere thanksgiving ever.

A NEW BEGINNING

One day I discussed Randy's mental state and development with an old friend, Joanna. I told her in a gloomy tone, "The doctors said this child is mentally retarded; I am afraid he that he won't be able to learn much." She answered, "Don't worry. God is the source of wisdom. We can ask Him for it."

Joanna's comments really encouraged me. I began to pray daily for heavenly wisdom from God for Randy, my family, and myself.

One day I was alone with Randy. I raised him up and knelt down praying to God: "Lord, when King Solomon became king he didn't ask anything else from you but WISDOM; you were pleased with his request and granted him wisdom unsurpassed by anyone. Now I present this child before you and ask you to give him not worldly wisdom but the heavenly wisdom that you have promised for him."

I often stared at Randy and told him, "Darling, remember one thing! God will give you the gift of wisdom because your mommy has already sent the request for you to God – the origin of wisdom. You and Mommy should both remember that. Don't you forget!"

Since then our house became a live classroom – with colorful pictures and writings everywhere. Furniture, headboard, walls, and staircases… all became Randy's teachers. Over the next six years our live classroom was upgraded from red, yellow, and blue into circles, triangles, and squares, then numbers and simple songs. I tried to talk to him every opportunity I got, even long before he could utter any words. That way he would get acquainted with many common terms. For example: "Randy, Mommy is giving you a bath. Look, water, this is water." I would also give him a drink of water from a cup and splash water on his cheeks. "Water... water... and water." It would be repeated at least a hundred times during a bath.

So we seized every opportunity to learn, even though it might be a minute or a second. Every day we would ask for God's wisdom and strength to help us – the same way for six years. Randy was struggling along, the progress being made slowly yet surely.

The seventy-two day hospitalization of Randy in the Infant Intensive Care Unit had given me a new beginning in my outlook on life. A hospital is a place with hope but also full of heart-breaking stories. During the seventy-two days, I'd seen the severely wounded survivors of automobile accidents who lost other family members. There were handicapped infants abandoned by their parents, and people who underwent brain surgery without relatives to care for them.... Suddenly I realized that the world is a composite of happiness and sadness. "Success" and "failure" may be extremes; yet "smooth sailing" and "hardship" do exist in parallel. "Life" and "death" are practically neighbors.

The "being unfortunate" philosophy may be looked at from both the positive and the negative sides. Some people give up easily and remain sad and miserable all their lives, while others persevere to the end, overcoming all kinds of hardships. The difference lies not only in one's determination to overcome but also in the source of inner strength, which can be the turning point of life.

I also believe that everyone likes accomplishments because they motivate people. Constant failure, on the other hand, can destroy the desire for living. These things are true for "normal people" as well as "abnormal people." The really smart people are satisfied with "big steps forward"; however, those with low intellect can attain the same degree of satisfaction with every "small step forward." Steps can be adjusted and divided so that the sense of accomplishment is not measured by the size of the step but by the efforts that are put into it.

There was an American philosopher, Dale Carnegie, whose books Clement and I love to read. He once said that it is not important what a person was born with, but it is very important to have the right attitude toward the conditions that life brings. For instance, it is sad to be born blind; but it would be even sadder if one did not have the ability to cope with it. Isn't the well-known story of Helen Keller a good example? I tend to agree with Carnegie's reasoning; however, human emotion is so unpredictable with highs and lows. It would be very difficult to pull oneself out of a "low-point" situation. In my own experience, I discovered that it was far better to draw my "energy" from the Creator and move on with my life than to rely on myself in the struggle against our unfortunate destiny.

Clement and I learned to cling onto this source of energy so that we could enjoy our three children, and endure unwanted criticism. More preciously, our family has learned the lesson of compassion, truly loving one another.

I remember an episode when Randy was about three

years old. The older boys were playing outside the front door with their friends. Randy wobbled over to the glass door and was looking out at them. Suddenly one of the kids asked my second son, Isaac, "Isaac, is this your… ah…. your dummy brother?" I overheard his question and was worried about Isaac's reaction. To my surprise, Isaac calmly opened the door, picked Randy up, and said with a smile, "This is my little brother. He learns things a bit slower, but he is lovely."

Then he put Randy down in the middle of his friends and showed him off: "See! He can smile, he can wave at you, he can…." All the kids were smiling and waving at Randy and had a marvelous time. As a bystander, I couldn't help but utter my thanksgiving to God: "Lord, I thank you for giving words of wisdom to Isaac, because he didn't deny his little brother's disability. Instead, he steered him in a firm and positive way."

We constantly paid attention to the two older boys to see how they cared for their "special" little brother. Clement repeatedly reminded me that Randy was our "challenge." If we handled Randy right, it would have a very positive and constructive impact on the two older boys. Based on this principle, Clement tried very hard to help me. We also remembered a warning from a social worker. She told me that many families with disabled children end up with problems among parents and siblings. So we were emotionally careful, being especially aware of the fragile bond that holds families together.

The two older boys soon learned to accept Randy in their lives. Whenever they were around friends, Randy was

85

one of the trio. They loved Randy and cared about his well-being. They even searched through medical books to gain more understanding of Randy's conditions. While doing homework, they often kept Randy nearby. He would try to scribble or draw on a piece of paper in imitation of his studious big brothers. Randy liked to be around when Geoffrey practiced clarinet or Isaac played piano. One day he even brought out his toy harmonica and indicated his intention to join Geoffrey and Isaac in a musical trio.

Love grew in our family and brought us ever closer, because we always went through the "better" and the "worse" situations together. We were very thankful the two older boys received baptism and publicly professed their Christian faith when Randy was about three years old. God taught us the essence of "LOVE" – "Giving first and receiving second." Randy was like a mirror: his face reflected the smiles that others gave him, and his closeness and affection showed the love he received.

"<u>God crowns the year with His grace</u>" is the precise description for the years that passed. It isn't easy to learn how to trust God. As in the case of a student enduring the learning processes, the homework, quiz, and exams bring on much pressure and fatigue. Even though he studies hard, he may still forget what he has learned and do poorly in the final tests. Yet at the end of the school year, he finds his knowledge has been broadened and his reading ability has improved. Progress has been made regardless of the ups and downs. God has set many milestones for our lives. After we reach the milestones and finish the journey according to His plans, He will reward us with "Crowns of Victory" for honoring His will and following it, so that we, the imperfect, can enter into His perfect glory.

The pastor of our church once told me he was "crazy about chocolate." One day he walked into the kitchen when his wife was preparing a chocolate cake. Out of curiosity he tasted all the ingredients individually. Oh, how awful! The chocolate powder was bitter; the butter was greasy; the eggs were raw; even the sugar didn't taste right. He would be completely wrong, though, if he concluded that the chocolate cake was inedible because all the ingredients didn't taste good. These ingredients, through the skillful hands of the baker and the baking process, could produce a delicious chocolate cake at the end.

Aren't life's ingredients acting in the same way? The Heavenly Creator is the Lord of my life. He is the potter and I am the clay. The value of life (as short as it is) lies in one's effort and contribution to God's plan. Children are the inheritance that God gives us, so that we can understand the eternal inheritance that He has prepared for all His believers (His children). This is the greatest blessing from God.

The days of life seem to pass by in a twinkle of an eye. As it says in the Bible, "We finish our years with a moan. The length of our days is seventy years – or eighty, if we have the strength; yet its span is but trouble and sorrow; for they quickly pass, and we fly away." Yes, life is brief, but those who believe in God's plan will not lose heart because of its shortness. Moses, one of the great men in the Bible, asked God to teach his heart so that he could carry out God's plan and glorify His name. God, indeed, blessed and affirmed the works accomplished through Moses.

This new stage of my life, with its pain and joy, confirmed to me the real value of life. We were living for God's pre-planned goal. Various aspects of life, such as work, family, children, and church all worked together and revolved around the center of our lives. Although there would be obstacles along the way, I firmly believe that God's grace is sufficient for us just like what this hymn says:

> "Many things about tomorrow, I don't seem to understand;
> But I know who holds tomorrow, and I know who holds my hand."

While I was writing this chapter, Randy approached me, climbed on my lap, and asked curiously, "Mommy, what are you doing?"

I put down the pen, held him, and said, "Oh, sweetheart, mommy is writing a story about you."

"About me?" He smiled but didn't really understand.

"Yes, about you, honey. It is also a story about God."

"About God?" He still didn't understand, but with a sweet smile he said, "Mommy, I love you," as he slipped down from me.

Then he walked toward the family room to play. Out of tune, he sang over and over the only phrase he could remember from a Psalm: "Hosanna, praise he the Lord…"

***The translation of <u>Child of Oriental Face</u> ends here.
The following chapters bring Randy's story up to date.***

LEARNING IS FUN

It was a warmer day in early March 1989. Though the ground was still covered by snow, I paced back and forth in the garden, looking for any sign of spring. After a long cold winter, I anticipated the arrival of spring.

Suddenly I saw a dark greenish dot appear in the midst of the white snow. It was the tip of a tulip that had probed through the frozen ground.

"Randy, Randy, tulips are coming out. Come and look!"

I bundled him up in his winter coat and shoes. Together, we searched for more tulip tips. Soon I found more: "One, two, three... ten... twenty... thirty...." Together we counted. I was sure that I could find more, since I had planted four hundred bulbs a few years ago.

"Randy, isn't it amazing that they all come out at the same time? They don't talk to each other, but they seem to know what to do. Isn't it wonderful?" I asked him.

Pointing at the tulip tips one by one, he tried to repeat what I said, "Won-doo-ful! Won-doo-ful!" He was engrossed in talking to the tulip tips. At age eight, his pronunciation was still somewhat unclear.

A few minutes later, he was still happily talking. Then, I noticed that he was saying something differently. Rather than saying "Wonderful! Wonderful!" he seemed to say, "Wake up! Wake up!"

"Randy, what did you say to those tulips? Did you say 'wake up, wake up'?" I looked at his smiling face, rosy and content.

"God said, 'Wake up! Y-o-u! Wake up!'" With one hand

holding onto mine, and another one pointing at the tulips, he continued to talk. I liked his blithe spirit and simple way of communicating with nature.

The time clock of nature was pre-programmed for all living things by the Creator. At the right time, right place, and the right condition, the living creatures respond to the codes imbedded within them.

I looked around my garden, and recalled those perennials Clement and I planted through the years. I knew that they would return in an orderly sequence with crocus and daffodils blossoming first; tulip, forsythia, iris, and peonies coming afterward. Early May is always my favorite time of the year. Our sixty azalea plants would blossom at the same time and provide the yard with bright red, pink, and white colors.

"There is a time for everything and a season for every activity under heaven." King Solomon had written this sentence in Ecclesiastes when he was old. "Y-o-u! Wake up! Y-o-u! Wake up!" Randy was still talking. I could only thank the Holy Spirit for communicating the message to his heart in such a special way. It was a gift of wisdom from the Creator.

I think wisdom is a source of truth that gives us the ability to synchronize with the Creator. Wisdom teaches a humble heart. It is a guiding light that leads to the discovery of the wonderful creation. It is like an unspoken breath unveiling the miracle to a meek seeker. Isaac Newton dedicated his life to learning about God and nature. He believed that in order to "truly know the Creator one must study the natural scheme of things – the original ordering of matter and the laws that govern its composition and motion."

Since we became parents, Clement and I have committed ourselves to bringing up our children in a godly way. We realized that the first thing we had to do was to establish a nest of love for each other and our children. We know that there is no greater gift we can give to our children than loving each other. It provides a secure and stable environment for our children. The experience of raising Randy enhanced our mission and goals. We believe that each person, regardless of his mental and physical conditions, has received special gifts from God. It is our job to bring forth the full potential of each member of the family. We have the responsibility to set the tone and the examples for our children to follow, so that they can accept and love one another unconditionally.

Every day brings us challenges, but it also brings us success. A positive family culture enriches the hearts of family members and encourages the desire to learn and to communicate our thoughts freely. It is always fun to talk, to learn, and to do things together. Communication brings our hearts and minds together.

The opportunities for teaching Randy exist frequently, but the key is to catch the right moment to explain the topic he is most interested in. In other words, the key is to "seize the moment." This sounds easy but it is not. It means everyone in the family must be sensible to the "moment" when it occurs. Everyone must store up a reservoir of ready-to-use knowledge and the willingness to look for more. This requires tremendous patience and analytical power to simplify a complicated fact without losing the essence of it. To develop the "skill of explaining things" is an art and a skill in itself.

Talking about "seizing the moment," I remember a great opportunity popped up one day when Randy was ten years old. Randy came home proudly with a deck of baseball cards that was awarded to him by his homeroom teacher for his persistent good behavior. With a pencil and paper, and fully concentrating, he copied down something from those cards over and over. I became curious. I asked him about what he had copied off the cards. He told me that he wanted to know each player's name, the team he belonged to, and the player's best score. For the next two evenings, he wrote and covered many sheets of paper and the entire white board with the baseball stuff. Obviously, he liked the baseball cards very much.

Observing this, I asked myself, "What can I do to take him beyond what he is already doing?"

Then an idea came to my mind. I realized that it was a wonderful opportunity to teach him how to organize information. Since Randy was familiar with a computer keyboard, showing him how to organize baseball card information on a computer was a logical thing to do.

First, I gave him three highlighters in different colors. I spent one evening with him to highlight the name of the player, the team, and the best score of each player in different colors for each card. Then, on the second evening, I created a database structure and showed him how to enter the data into the database. It took us a few days to complete all the data entry. Then I showed him how to use a printer to create a "card list." I even showed him how to sort the list into a specific order. Since he loved these cards so much, he listened to me carefully and had all the motivation to learn. After he enjoyed his computerized "baseball card system" for a few days, I asked him, "Randy, can you tell me from the computer how many players in your card deck belong to the Baltimore Orioles?" With little hints, he said, "I think I can sort by team. They will be together." He logged on to the computer and brought back a sorted printout with Baltimore Orioles players grouped together. He told me that there were six Orioles players. I asked him a few more questions, such as "Who has the best score?" "How many players' names start with the letter W?" I was overjoyed when he figured out how to utilize the database to answer my questions. I told him that I was proud of him, and I would buy more baseball cards for him. I did and he continued to maintain this database for over a year.

I had seized the moment to teach him an important lesson. The process helped him to organize scattered raw data into useful information. I found that this little success carried him a long way toward later learnings.

Life is a school. Everyday it brings us special lessons. Our abilities are challenged through those lessons that demand our responses and actions. Children learn to meet those challenges through responsibilities. President Theodore Roosevelt once said, "Your ability needs responsibility to expose its possibilities. Do what you can with what you have where you are." As parents, we have the obligation to instill and implement this concept into our children's hearts.

Light Into Dawn – Randy's Miracle

I feel that the biggest privilege, and the best part of being a parent, is to explore our children's potentials, to harness those potentials, and to maintain them. Those potentials are gifts from God. They are abilities in the dormant stage. It is important for parents to look beyond the seeds, plant them in a good environment and cultivate them, so that the children can fulfill their life goals. God gives us children; He wants us to raise them and enjoy them. He also wants us to grow with our children in the "school of life." This does not mean that we have all the answers for our children. It means we, as parents, have the responsibility to do our best to pool necessary resources together for the well-being of our children.

I learned a new term called "synergy" at my workplace several years ago. I believe that this term has a perfect application in our family life. What is synergy? As a result of people working together, the product is greater than the sum of components. For example, mathematically, we all know that one plus one equals two. However, with synergy, the result can be greater than two. In Randy's case, I realize that teaching him is a long-term job. We need to "energize" all possible resources together as a team.

I thought about Helen Keller's story that I read when I was a teenager. Helen was born on June 27, 1880, in Alabama. She had been a healthy child until age two. She caught a fever that was so fierce she nearly died. She survived but she became blind, deaf, and mute. Helen was frustrated. She kicked and screamed all the time. Finally, just before her seventh birthday, the family hired a tutor, Anne Sullivan. Miss Sullivan taught Helen to communicate, to read, and to write. Miss Sullivan was so creative that she taught Helen more than anyone could imagine. She accompanied Helen through daily living, high school, and finally, in 1904, through her graduation with honors from Radcliffe College.

Without Miss Sullivan, Helen probably would have remained a pitiful, mixed-up person, who could not see, hear, or talk. Miss Sullivan dug into the potential hidden deeply inside Helen, dragged it out, and helped her to see beyond her eyes, to hear beyond her ears, and to communicate beyond her mouth. Miss Sullivan and Helen had "synergized" together to bring forth Helen's potential.

"I need a Miss Sullivan for Randy," I said to myself. As matter of fact, I knew I needed more than one Miss Sullivan to do the job. So, I prayed hard everyday and asked God to send "Miss Sullivans" to Randy's life. I started to work very closely with all his teachers. I started to look at Randy's education from a different perspective. Rather than just "sending" Randy to school, I looked at myself as the person responsible for managing Randy's education. Teachers and I became a team. Together, we made a joint effort to cultivate Randy's potential.

Through the years, I witnessed the result of this synergizing effect. It was fun to work with a team of God-sent "Miss Sullivans." Mrs. Brooks and Mrs. Reihm started the engine in Randy's life, in the early intervention program when Randy was only eleven months old. Mrs. Venderwende, a lovely Christian lady, opened the world of communication by teaching Randy sign language and better verbal expression. Mrs. Cox taught Randy to paddle a tricycle and to swim. Mrs. Palmer ran the first science lab with Randy. Together he and she hatched a baby chick, and she allowed Randy to bring it home. (Eventually, it grew into a big rooster, and its crow became a disturbance for our neighbors. My husband had to send it away.) Mrs. Frazier was the catalyst for the "turning point" in Randy's education. She insisted that Randy be mainstreamed, and she took the initiative to transfer Randy into a regular elementary education. After Randy was placed in the regular public school, Miss White, Mrs. Foltz, and Mrs. Zimmerman went over and above their normal obligations and helped him a great deal. Mrs. Frazier also gave Randy every possible opportunity to perform his freshly learned piano pieces. She nominated Randy to perform at the International Very Special Arts concert in 1994. After he auditioned, her nomination was accepted, and Randy represented the State of Delaware by performing at the Royal Museum in Brussels, Belgium.

When Randy started junior high, we realized that his poor eyesight had become a problem for him in seeing the blackboard. His weak balancing ability limited his mobility in school. Besides, we really wanted to instill him with strong Christian values. With everything considered, we decided to transfer him to a Christian school under a self-paced program.

It has proven to be a correct decision. The new "Miss Sullivans" in the Christian school brought Randy to a higher ground both academically and spiritually. He was loved, cared for, and nurtured by a team of teachers who work in harmony with me, to bring out the deep potential within him.

Another "Miss Sullivan" in Randy's life is his piano teacher, Tracy. Tracy is Randy's mentor, his best friend and coach. There is no one who understands the gift of music that God gave to Randy better than Tracy does. Always encouraging, always positive, always graceful, Tracy patiently cultivates an uncharted wealth. Tracy is a great performer herself, yet she has ways to communicate with Randy's thirst for music. Little by little, lesson after lesson, she plowed through Randy's hidden mind, planting seeds of music discipline. Together, they laugh, they hug, they struggle, and they harvest. Randy admires Tracy, and often he says, "Monday is the best day of the week, because I go to see Tracy."

Learning is fun! The culture we established for our family has been working for the past seventeen years, and I know it will continue to work.

Recapping my philosophy of education, I have shared the following basic ideas:

1. Be creative, and connect your creativity to the origin of creation.
2. Seize the moment. Don't let a good learning opportunity walk away unattended.
3. Determine to maximize abilities by exploring, harnessing, and maintaining the potentials.
4. Synergize all the resources together. "Togetherness" is the key.

God gives each one of us a different curriculum in the "school of life". The personalized lessons require us to take different paths to learn them. Nevertheless He gives us sufficient wisdom to accomplish them. There is a Bible verse that I highlighted in my Bible. Hebrew 12:1 advises us to "run with perseverance the race marked out for us...." I personalized the verse by writing the word "**me**" above the word "us". I believe the "race" is an individualized assignment. It is not meant to be compared with others. God has promised us that He will never give us a situation more than we can handle. He created each one of us with potentials, and he also promised each one of us abilities to fulfill those potentials.

Learning is fun. I have harvested some of the fruits of learning in my home. Through the process, I learned to teach, to love, and to look into the potential of my husband, my children, and myself. Life is a school. Challenges open opportunities to grow. Our family has been blessed by learning and growing together.

NOTES AND COUNTING

"Hmm, Mom, you have the same problem as I do — notes and counting," Randy once commented after my taking a voice lesson. But first some background to that remark:

Randy was nine years old when both his brothers, Geoffrey and Isaac, had left for college. An "empty nest" feeling crept in. I missed their piano and clarinet sounds. For many years, we had indulged ourselves in the free concert they provided every evening. Now the melody ceased. Our house seemed quiet and strange. Though we have over 9,000 classical music recordings, it was not the same as listening to live concerts.

On a quiet evening, I listened to Weber's Concerto No. 1 in F Minor, a clarinet-piano duet recording done by my two older sons a few years ago. Randy sat by me enjoying his crayon coloring.

"That's Geoffrey and Isaac playing!" said Randy excitedly, "Maybe I can play like them someday!"

A thought, actually a guilty feeling, rushed through my mind, "Why not him? I have not given him any chance to try, yet. But can he do it? Who will be willing to teach him?"

"Do you think you'd like to learn piano?" I asked Randy.

With a big smile on his face, he said, "Piano? Yes, Mommy!"

Oh, Lord! What could I do? I was standing at the crossroads now. Should I or shouldn't I? Was I dreaming about something that could never come true? Where should

Light Into Dawn – Randy's Miracle

I start? Then, I thought about the famous sentence Anatole France once said, "To accomplish great things, we must not only act but also dream, not only plan, but also believe." I told myself that maybe, just maybe, he will sense the beauty of the music when the tuning fork in his mind hums with the vibration of the piano strings.

With a vague idea, I took the first step. I discussed the thought with my husband and my two older sons. We agreed that we should try. The most important thing was to find a qualified teacher who had all the patience Randy needed. Based on our previous experience, unanimously, we felt that Wilmington Music School was the best choice. The school is located fifty miles from our home, but it was most likely to have all the components we needed. A few days later, I carefully wrote a letter to the school seeking a commitment and a partnership in this adventure. I was overjoyed when the school decided to accept Randy for his piano lessons. In order to make our weekly trips more worthwhile, I decided to sign up for voice lessons. Randy welcomed the idea because he wanted his mommy to attend the same school with him.

Soon after he started his piano lessons, our excitement was challenged by reality. I found that Randy's hand-eye coordination was very poor. It was questionable in my mind if he could actually distinguish a line from a space on the music staff. The progress in the first three months was rather slow. Once again, I was in the crossroads. Should we continue? Is it going to work?

Despite what I felt, Randy tried very hard to practice. Everyday I sat by him. We struggled through every note and every counting together. One evening, at the end of his twenty-minute practice, we engaged in an interesting conversation.

"I am a-l-l done, Mommy!" Randy raised his two hands and declared.

"Randy, you know what? You are doing better today then yesterday." I patted his back and tried to give him a few words of encouragement.

"B-e-t-t-e-r?" He looked at me, grinning from ear to ear.

"Yes, you are. Do you know why?" I asked.

"Is that because I practiced yesterday?"

"Yes, you are a-b-s-o-l-u-t-e-l-y right," I answered him. Suddenly I saw an unusual expression on his face. He gazed at the music in front of him. He looked solemn but lost. I tried to read his mind. "Are you OK?" I asked. "Mommy, will I be better tomorrow?" he asked slowly.

I was shocked. I could never have expected such a question from him.

"Yes, honey. You sure will."

I was still trying to figure out what was going through his mind.

"I will?" he said.

"Do you know why?" I asked but did not expect any straightforward answer.

"Is it because I practiced today?" he said and turned his face toward me.

"Yes, you are right, sweetheart," I answered, touching his curious face with my two hands.

Randy left the piano and went to get his reward for the

day – banana ice cream. While he was gone, I sat alone, staring at the piano notes. Tears streamed down my face. "Yes, I must continue the lessons! There is hope!" I thought to myself.

It was a night during which I lost some sleep. I pondered every word said in our conversation. I searched in my heart for the essence of "HOPE." I recalled that a Southern writer, Debbie Wilson, once said, "Hope is the opposite of despair. Hope is the opposite of discouragement. Hope is the opposite of impossible. Hope is the desire to overcome the odds. Hope comes from within the heart and soul. Hope is striving to be as successful as possible. Hope … is what carries us, when we are too tired to go on…. Hope's going forward, even when it hurts. Hope is the expectation that things will indeed get better…."

More than often, I had "wished" he could play an instrument. Now I realized that I had to go beyond wishing. A wish is desire without expectation, but hope comes with expectations. It was the expectation of a better tomorrow that drove this child to endure the hardship day after day. Wasn't it the same faculty of faith and hope that gave the early church and many missionaries their vigor and determination? As Apostle Paul said, "For I consider that the sufferings of this present time are not worthy to be compared with the glory which shall be revealed in us." It is the hope for a better tomorrow that made everything happen.

I created a slogan for him: "Little by little, day by day, better and better." We recited it every day before and after the piano practice. Gradually I realized that smoother melodies started to form. Randy's mind and music became closer. He was enchanted by the stories behind the music and became emotionally attached to the composers. The world in his mind was expanding. The tuning fork in his mind started to hum with the composer's notes. He felt proud of himself and wanted to know more. As Helen Keller once said, "One can never consent to creep when one feels an impulse to soar." Not only his musical sensibility increased, his musical aptitude actually improved.

One year after his music lesson, he presented two simple pieces at a school Christmas program. This event was the first of his many public appearances. Three years later, at age thirteen, he was selected by the Very Special Arts of Delaware to represent our state at the International Special Arts Celebration, and he performed at the Royal Museum in Brussels, Belgium. On a live TV performance, he played his heart out for a fund-raising event sponsored by Easter Seals. It was a moving experience to see $12,000 pledged by the public during that hour. All the money was used to help other children who had disabilities. In 1995 Randy received the Delaware Governor's Youth Volunteer Service Award for using his ability to help others. This experience gave him the satisfaction of being a giver rather than a recipient. Music was his vehicle.

Through the discipline of music, I also observed his intellectual maturation. I have no doubt in my mind that music has contributed to the general growth of this child. It molded his abilities in mind, body, and emotion into an integrated expressible form. Music is a social art. It brought him a rich sense of social participation, starting in our family circle. It provided him a social status among his friends. His power of attention expanded tremendously. His ability to concentrate and the desire to comprehend applied to every aspect of learning. As confidence and self-esteem became stronger and stronger, he was not afraid of learning difficult concepts any more. As he said often, "It is not hard. I just need to do it little by little." It became my constant challenge to figure out how to break down a difficult task into "little" pieces, string them together, and make the whole concept comprehensible to his eager mind. We face a formidable amount of work all the time. Nevertheless, through the labor, we harvest our fruit. Bob Greene, a writer, once said, "Work is a mysterious thing. Many of us claim to hate it, but it takes a grip on us that is so fierce that it captures emotions and loyalties we never knew were there." When the result of the work satisfies our inward desire, the effort to accomplish the goal becomes a willful process.

There is a quote I like. I made a copy and pasted it next to my computer at work. It says:

> When the pathway seems long,
> When temptation is strong,
> When your strength's almost gone,
> That's the time to press on.
> - Hess

We conquer by continuing. Notes and counting have become a common bound between Randy and me.

"THE WATER WHEEL"

If anyone has struggled to articulate a second language, he or she can certainly appreciate the efforts required. The term "articulation" refers to the speech sounds that are produced to form the words of language. The instruments of articulation are the lips, tongue, teeth, jaw, and palate. For some people who were born with a congenital disability, speaking may become a lifetime challenge.

Randy was born with an arched palate, a typical mouth structure for many Down's Syndrome people. Consequently, the pitch and quality are altered. For many years, Randy received speech therapy, and his pronunciation became better. Nevertheless, it was far from the level classified as "easy to be understood" by listeners.

When he was eleven, I determined to improve his pronunciation further, as well as his ability to express himself. I believed that the best way to accomplish my goal was to give him more opportunities to speak in front of people. I encouraged him to speak publicly whenever he had a chance to perform piano. Since he loved to perform, "speaking" became part of the deal.

"A thousand-mile journey begins with the first step." A short speech with a few sentences was all we needed. On a piece of paper, we wrote down the following words,

> "When I was a little baby, the doctor told my parents I may not be able to do many things. Praise the Lord! Now, I can play piano for you. Thank you."

We recorded this short speech, listened to it, and

practiced it over and over. By listening to his own recording, he was convinced that he could use some better pronunciation techniques. I corrected him syllable by syllable, word by word, and sentence by sentence. Through a long period of time, a better and clearer sound pattern started to form.

As his articulation improved, we added more sentences. The contents were expanded creatively by adding thoughts and activities that he could associate. It was an intense but interesting project that lasted more then three years. Our efforts were fruitful. Gradually Randy became confident in public speaking, and his pronunciation was much easier understood.

On June 23, 1995, he was invited by the Delaware Blue and Gold Team as the keynote speaker at their banquet to honor the high-school football stars and their efforts in helping handicapped children. In 1996 he was one of the feature speakers for the Delaware Boys and Girls Club. He shared the podium with U.S. Senator Joseph Biden and was honored as a role model.

The following speech has been delivered to more than two thousand people on various occasions. The text and the philosophy of the content are dear to Randy, and I feel that this book would be incomplete without including it.

God has blessed a child who seemed imperfect from a human standpoint, and God has included him in His perfect plan. We, as parents, are merely the instruments of delivering God's love, we do our best, and we "run with endurance the race that is set before us." Life is a school, from which we learn to minister and to serve.

"The Water Wheel"

— Randy Chang

Hello, everybody! I am glad to be here today. The Lord has done many special things in my special life. I'd like to share them with you.

Some of you may have heard that I like to play piano. One of my favorite pieces is called "The Water Wheel." As matter of fact, my piano teacher said that was my "signature piece." Well, one day my mom asked me, "Randy, do you really know what a water wheel is?" I said, "not really." So my mom said, "Ok, let's look it up in the encyclopedia and build a water wheel from Lego.

My mom helped me to build a wheelhouse by using all the wheels I could find from my Lego box, and we built a wheelhouse. I put the wheelhouse under the kitchen faucet, and here came the fun part. I turned on the water and had water flowing over the wheels. Amazingly, they all worked. I was so excited.

Then, my mom and I had an interesting conversation. Through the conversation, I was inspired by the water wheel. I started to associate my own life with the water wheel.

When I was a little tiny baby, I was so sick. I had organ disorders, and doctors told my parents that I have Down's Syndrome. I went through six major surgeries and was in the infant intensive care for seventy-two days. During this time, the doctor told them I might not live. If I survived, I may not learn; I may not even be able to take care of myself. My parents were so sad. But my parents did not give up. They believed

107

that the God they believe in is the source of wisdom, the source of power, and from Him, there is a s-t-r-e-a-m of Living Water.

In the past seventeen years, my parents prayed very hard and worked very hard with me. They set me under this Living Water and taught me to rely on a power which is bigger than myself. Every morning I memorize and meditate on Bible verses. Through the day, I feel the joy of learning. At night, I thank Him for the strength He gave me for that day. At times, I have difficulties, but I know I'll be okay because I am powered by the Living Water.

This Living Water gives me hope. Every day I believe that today I am doing better than yesterday, because I worked hard yesterday. Tomorrow, I will be better than today, because I worked hard today. I am content with what God has given me, because I know He can easily bless me with more.

I thank God for the gifts he gave me. He gave me music in my hands. I love to share it with people, because music makes me happy, music helps other people be happy, and people make me happy.

Let me tell you another story. In May 1994 I represented the State of Delaware by performing piano in Brussels, Belgium, at the International Very Special Arts Celebration. During that week, I met eight hundred people from seventy-two different countries and states. I heard the most sophisticated music played by a violinist who was born without an inner and outer ear. I saw the finest drawing that was made by a person who was paralyzed from his neck down. I saw the most beautiful dance performed by deaf people.

I want to tell you about a special lady I met. Right after my performance, when I walked off the stage, a lady moved *her wheelchair towards me. She told me her name was Kitty Lynn, and she had been an actress for a TV show called "As the World Turns" before she became paralyzed. Kitty held my hand, and said, "Randy, I want you to remember this: A miracle is not for me to get out of this wheelchair. A miracle is not for you to throw away your Down's Syndrome. Rather, a miracle is when other people realize what we can do and they start to know us better."*

I believe in miracles. What's a miracle? I fully agree with what Kitty said: "A miracle is not for my disability to go away. A miracle happens when we give ability a chance."

Ability is powered by energy. Where does the energy come from? The energy is generated by connecting myself to the Living Water.

I am a simple water wheel. It may be small. It may be imperfect. It is only an instrument. But the little wheel is willing. As long as the Living Water keeps flowing on the wheel, the wheel will keep on spinning, and I believe that the miracle will keep on happening.

I'd like to share with you a Bible verse I memorized: "I can do all things in Christ, which strengtheneth me" (Philippians 4:13).

A water wheel without water cannot spin;
A seed without life cannot sprout; and
A sinner without salvation cannot be saved.

Praise the Lord!
With the Living Water, a simple water wheel can spin;
With the energy of life, a seed can grow; and

Light Into Dawn – Randy's Miracle

With the salvation of Jesus, we can receive redemption.

I am glad I am studying in a Christian school. There is a neat, wise saying I learned from my textbook. I want to share with you. It says: "Our faultless Savior saw our fall, and bought our pardon on the cross." By the redemption of Jesus Christ, I am saved; I am living; and I am happy. WHY? Because I have gotten the most important thing of my life – Jesus Christ, the Living Water that powers me.

May God have all his honor and Glory, for He loves us so much.

Thank you.

NOTES/ COMMENTS

This book is a testimonial to a family that believes that with the help and guidance of God, all things are possible. The faith and personal commitment of the Chang family is a reminder that God delights in doing that which seems to be impossible. God also delights in individuals who stretch to the limit their abilities and then wait upon God for a life's journey that takes them beyond. Randy's life is an ongoing witness to a God who loves and is able. Here's another hug to you Randy, keep on reaching!

– Dr. Richard L. Nelson, pastor
First Baptist Church
Dover, Delaware

It is a pleasure to support the efforts of the Chang Family in sharing their story. The family truly exemplifies the logo of Very Special Arts which is "Promoting the creative and artistic power in people with disabilities." This family has integrated and used the arts... especially music... to bond as a family, to teach patience and perseverance, to share memories and moments, and to prove that ALL can find expression through the arts. Randy and his family have opened doors throughout the community and demonstrate that their faith, family values, and caring spirit can conquer any adversity. This story will remind all that family togetherness can maximize abilities and that every moment is a learning opportunity.

– Jennifer Taylor
15-year Executive Director
of Very Special Arts - DE

Light Into Dawn – Randy's Miracle

This heart-rending narrative of Bethel's, and her family's trials after the birth of Randy epitomizes the healing power of their faith. Randy is not only a joy to his parents but to all who have the good fortune to know him.

– Rick Collin
Friend of the family